The Ascent and fragmenta

professional coaching ass

Table of Contents

INTRODUCTION 3
THE PIONEERING STAGE OF PROFESSIONAL COACHING ASSOCIATIONS 5
    SOLIDIFYING OF EARLY LEADERSHIP ROLES 11
    THE ADOPTION OF EXISTING ORGANISATION FORMS AND STRUCTURES 13
    ABSENCE OF EXTERNAL REGULATION – THE FATAL FLAW 14
    THE SOCIAL CONSTRUCTION OF CELEBRITY COACHES AMONG THE LEADERSHIP 17
    MANUFACTURING THE 'VOLUNTEER DEFENCE.' 20
    IS COACHING INTRINSICALLY VIRTUOUS? 22
    DOWNSIDES OF PROFESSIONALISING 25

GOVERNANCE AND CONTROL THROUGH 'PSEUDO-REGULATION' 28
    THE CREATION OF HYPERREALITY THROUGH MARKETING HYPE 35

POWER, CONTROL AND 'VIRTUAL OWNERSHIP' AMONG COACHING ASSOCIATIONS 37
    THE PLAYING OUT OF NEO-FEUDALISM AMONG COACHING ASSOCIATIONS 41

BRAND BUILDING AROUND CELEBRITY COACHES' PERSONAS. ... 45
    NAVIGATING THE 'FOUNDER'S DILEMMA.' 46
    CREATING A 'MESSIAH COMPLEX' TO CULTIVATE CULT-LIKE CULTURES 48

THE 'ACCREDITATION' INFLECTION POINT 50
    PULLING UP THE DRAWBRIDGE ON THE EMANCIPATORY IMPULSE. 52
    ACCREDITATION DRIVES ELITISM THROUGH DESENSITISATION. 56
    ESPOUSING ETHICAL CODES AS A PROXY FOR EXTERNAL REGULATION. 59
    'CONTENT' PROVIDERS ROLES IN THE ACCREDITATION ECO-SYSTEM. 61
    COUNTERING POTENTIAL NEWBIES OBJECTIONS TO THE ACCREDITATION SALES PITCH 63
    COACHING COMMISSIONERS LEGITIMISE ACCREDITATION OVER MERE MEMBERSHIP. 65
    NICHE COACHING ASSOCIATIONS CONFORMING TO ACCREDITATION TROPES 68

RADICAL NETWORKS CANNOT RESIST THE SOLIDIFYING 'INSTITUTE' SIGNIFIER. 69
BUSINESS EXECUTIVES AND ASSOCIATION LEADERS IN COMMON CAUSE. 71
THE SUGGESTIVE POWER OF FOUNDATION STORIES. 78
WHAT DIFFERENT TYPES OF CREDENTIAL CONSUMER ARE THERE? 87
THE CREDENTIALS 'ARMS RACE:' PREMATURE SELLING OF NOVEL PRODUCTS. 95
QUANTITY TRUMPING QUALITY IN COACHING ASSOCIATIONS' PRIORITIES. 99
REFLECTIVE PRACTICE ENDANGERED BY SPEED-LEARNING IMPERATIVES. 105
THE IMPACT OF DIGITALISATION ON CENTRALISATION OF CONTROL 111
INFANTILISATION AND CREATION OF A FEAR CULTURE 114
ENTERING THE MATURATION STAGE OF ASSOCIATION DEVELOPMENT. 119
   THE REALITY BEHIND DEPENDENCE ON A VOLUNTEER BASE 119
   COUNTERING THE VOLUNTEERISM DEFENCE: UNMASKING HIGH CONTROL TACTICS 121
   THE VOLUNTEER JUSTIFICATION: FOSTERING RELATIONAL EXCHANGES OVER TRANSACTIONAL 124
   AT WHAT POINT DOES THE LOYALTY OF VOLUNTEERS SNAP? 127
   HUBRIS CAUSING LEADERS FAILING TO DETECT THE VOLUNTEER TIPPING POINT 129

DEEPENING THE JOURNEY INTO THE LATER MATURATION STAGE FOR ASSOCIATIONS 132
   COLONISATION STRATEGIES: AN ETHICAL ANALYSIS 140

FOLLOW THE MONEY – PULLING BACK THE CURTAIN 144
FACING SQUEEZES ON COACHES' DISCRETIONARY SPEND. 149
OPPORTUNITY COST IMPACT CAUSING COACHES TO ABANDON SHIP 152
EARLY DECLINE AND FRAGMENTATION STAGE 157
   CHALLENGES TO THE VOLUNTEER DEFENCE 165
   VOLUNTEERS STRUGGLES IN THE FACE OF DIGITALISATION OF MEMBER SERVICES. 169

ESPOUSED ETHICS AND ETHICS IN PRACTICE 173
    THE ABSENCE OF INFORMED CONSENT WHILE MARKETING AND GROWING
    COACHING ASSOCIATIONS 174
    WHEN COACHING ASSOCIATION LEADERS DO NOT HOLDING THEIR OWN
    ACCREDITATIONS. 175
    THE BURIAL OF EXECUTIVE COACHES' METAPHORICAL DEAD 179
    WHISTLEBLOWING 182

RESEARCH – A PERFORMATIVE APPROACH? 184
    DO COACHING ASSOCIATIONS VALORISE CONFIRMATION DATA WHILE
    VIGOROUSLY SUPPRESSING DISCONFIRMING INFORMATION? 190

**TWO-WAY TRAFFIC BETWEEN BUSINESS SCHOOLS AND
COACHING ASSOCIATIONS 195**
    THE EMERGENCE OF SCHOLAR-PRACTITIONERS ON THE CREDENTIALS
    LANDSCAPE. 198

**THE RISE OF BULLSHIT JOBS WITHIN COACHING ASSOCIATIONS
.... 204**

FEAR OF INTIMACY AND OF UNKNOWING 209

**JUMPING ON THE VIRTUE SIGNALLING AND GREENWASHING
BANDWAGONS 217**

DECLINE, RENEWAL AND REINVENTION 220

Introduction

The focus of this book is almost exclusively on the ascent then fragmentation of professional coaching associations over the past thirty years. It makes glancing reference to the emergence and proliferation of 'life coaching,' which has exploded across the western world, though the influence of life coaching's central focus on positive psychology upon the development of professional coaching is noted. It seeks to serve as a critical perspective on a narrative that is mostly told by the associations themselves, whose unsurprising tendency is to valorise their own ascension.

Dr Daniel Doherty has worked in and around the professional coaching world for nearly fifty years, both as practitioner and critical academic researcher, and commentator and activist in the field, challenging professional coaching associations' basic assumptions from an insider positioning. Daniel has led the Critical Coaching Group in the UK since 2006, which continues to cast a critical eye on developments within coaching, including the influence of the professional associations. Given this European positioning, then the sources drawn upon in the development of the arguments contained in this text tend to be more concentrated on European based coaching associations rather than the USA ones. However, given the fact that the USA has continued to be a front runner in setting the tone and offering templates for associations' development, then the fingerprint of USA influence on European developments is detectable throughout this book.

The pioneering stage of professional coaching associations

Professional coaching associations did not appear out of nowhere. They were not brought down from the mountain by a beneficent management guru, nor were they ushered in by a corporate lightning bolt. Contrary to the foundation stories which suggested that professional coaching associations had experienced a simultaneous virgin birth at some point in the late 1990s, the fact remains that the birth of professional coaching and its host associations have many antecedents in the pre-existing 1990s network of management consultants, leadership gurus and personal life coaches. The pivot towards executive coaching came in part from a widespread disenchantment with one-size-fits-all leadership and management training, which had outlived its novelty value, not least when it was revealed that executives displaying the capacity to survive in the great outdoors through the building of rafts, as a proxy for running major corporations had had its day.

The creation of parasitic professional coaching associations relied on, as their host, the burgeoning growth of the market for executive coaching which emerged during the mid to late

1990s and beyond, when executive coaching in its early days was often positioned as a highly virtuous activity that had at its centre an emancipatory impulse. The growth in the number of coaching practitioners grew in parallel with this faddish wave that placed executive coaching as the latest must-have conspicuous consumption item for in-the-know executives. Those coaches who jumped in, feet first, at the beginning of this wave did not take long to envision the need for some degree of shaping of this burgeoning practice/profession into a recognisable social construct that followers would flock towards.

Before asking what might be driving the demand for Coaching Associations, we need first to first what is it that drives the practice of coaching, without which there would be no market for such associations, as coaching practice is the host upon which these self-styled professional associations feed.

The demand for executive coaches can be attributed in part to the fulfilment of fundamental human need for self-improvement, guidance and mentorship, emotional support, and a sense of belonging - ,and executive coaches fulfil these needs in a professional context. While it is often assumed that executives seek coaching solely to enhance their leadership skills or overcome specific challenges in their professions, there are deeper unspoken psychological, emotional, and between their skill-set and executive demand, just at the point when their traditional training based, massified markets for off-the-job training were at saturation point, and probably peaking.

For many of these newly badged coaches, they discovered that engagement with the process of supporting isolated clients brought to the surface these coaches' own struggles with isolation. It gave rise to their reciprocal yearning for a sense of belonging to a recognisable tribe, in association with like-minded others. As independent professionals, they frequently lacked a robust support network, and they felt that lack acutely, especially in comparison with their corporate clients, who inhabited structures and hierarchies that provided a strong sense of purpose and belonging – even if these structures were not always conducive to mental health.

This search for informal collegiality, the need for coaches to connect with like-minded professionals, sharing experiences, knowledge, and support drove demand for the emergence of a variety of forms of coaching association. Beyond the need to build a social identity, a significant factor that was driving the demand was the need for professional respectability and legitimacy. As the industry matured, so clients and organisations sought coaches with credible credentials, and established methodologies.

This scramble for the formation of recognisable coaching associations witnessed leaders stepping up within these early, loosely formed coaching support groups and associations. These leaders sought to establish themselves as influential figures within the coaching industry and across commercial markets more broadly. While the drive for association was often built upon a conscious emancipatory impulse to make self-development available to all, the demand for coaching association aided a number of these leaders in achieving their own emergent ambitions, as they served as a platform to showcase their expertise, build networks, and gain recognition, as well as for seeking individual financial reward.

In this way the natural coalescence of coaching leaders with their followers began. Even in the early stages, the latent tensions inherent in some leaders prioritising self-promotion over the ethical responsibility or emancipation were apparent. The fusion of coaches' needs for a sense of belonging, and the ego-driven aspirations of coaching association leaders clearly held in the crucible the potential for creating a febrile, contended environment. As their followers grew in number, then the leaders could see a market in catering not only to coach's basic needs for affiliation. They could also visualise a window opening for mining needs that coaches did not even know they needed at that point, such as the need for professional legitimacy, and personal competency and mastery.

This drive for the formation of organisational identity was proving successful in legitimatised these coaching associations while to some extent closing off challenges to this emergent orthodoxy. The implications of this fast-growing ascent raised some scepticism regarding the capacity for exploitation among these executive coaching associations as they trawled the executive coaching industry for opportunities for marketing and growth.

As these associations grew and matured, they provided platforms, such as networking events, conferences, and online forums, to facilitate connections between their members, by means of fostering a sense of belonging, Their offer was to prioritise creating safe and non-judgmental environments where coaches could openly discuss their challenges, aspirations, and vulnerabilities, allowing coaches to feel accepted and understood.

Solidifying of early leadership roles

As the identity of these associations solidified, so too did the leaders' roles gain in substance, to the point where they were spending as much time proselytising their professional association and teaching coaching skills as they were actually doing one-on-one coaching. In this way they were able to step aside from direct coaching- a market that was already reaching saturation point – to concentrate on carving out a role for themselves servicing the needs of their coach members.

Many of these early adopters envisaged a rich opportunity accruing from them being poised at the front of that wave as the shapers of an emergent profession. For some, their desire was to be positioned as messianic pioneers of a person-centred wave, where they drew upon and extended their background in therapeutic counselling, drawing upon Rogerian principles such as non-directive 'unconditional positive regard', where you 'start where the client is at.' Such pioneers were visualising professional coaching as no less than a vocation, a calling to liberate executive clients from oppressive corporate mindsets and systems restrictions, while also working towards the more ambitious agenda of emancipating the organisations within which their clients were entrapped (albeit comfortably so, in the lucrative sense, locked into the golden handcuffs).

Other newly badged, less altruistically inclined coaching practitioners sensed that there were commercial gains to be made from taking a lead in the formation of associations for coaching practitioners which would provide shape and coherence to this fledgling profession, based on the real enough evidence of the highly human need for practitioners to cluster together in what can be a lonely and ill-defined field. These early pioneers were finding each other informally, relishing precious time together to share client-side experiences, to provide listening and support, and also to talk over ways to build viable businesses in this nascent field. Given this need, these early practitioners responded eagerly to the offering of a professional place for them to belong, within which they would be formally recognised and given a distinct identity as they sought to develop their credibility and widen their customer base. As momentum grew for associations, the burgeoning excitement attendant on being in at the beginning, at basement level, of something new that could only grow and solidify over the years, was palpable.

The adoption of existing organisation forms and structures

As these professional coaching associations came into being, it is hardly surprising that, as they sought legitimisation, they took as their template the structures and governance practises of well-established professions such as accountancy, the law, medicine, counselling, even HR, which had in the nineties enshrined itself in the UK within the exhaled status of a Royal Charter. In the late 1990s there were a number of such associations emerging around the world, most notably in the USA, the UK, and western Europe, with each working to attract members through their claims of professionalisation that would both protect and promote their members. As each association developed, they opted for similar governance structures and processes, expostulating the need for the regulation of practitioners to keep out the 'cowboys,' and for some form of accreditation and credentialing to allow potential buyers of these services to discriminate between the good, the bad and the ugly that prowled and circled around what none other than the Harvard Business School titled the 'wild west of coaching.' Perhaps these early, association building settlers saw themselves as a civilising counterpoint to cowboy lawlessness.

Absence of external regulation – the fatal flaw

While these associations' respective codes of practice were replete with fine sounding phrasing which lent a professional patina to their self-presentation, there was one fatal flaw that distinguished these bodies from those other professions they were seeking to emulate. And that flaw was that, despite their best efforts, these bodies could not claim that their members would be subject to external regulation in the same manner as established professions, by governmental bodies or academic institutions, either at the local or global level.

From these early pioneering beginnings in the nineties, the coaching industry has undergone a process of 'professionalisation' through various initiatives aimed at establishing standards, ethics, and accountability, as well as providing legitimised platforms for the monetisation of naturalistic coaching practice. This professionalising pathway has followed the professional templates for long-established professions such as medicine, accountancy, or the law; and in many ways mirrored the professionalising pathways of various mental health and counselling practices. The adoption of recognisable characteristics of professionalisation assisted including training of members and codes of conduct allowed coaching to outwardly project all the signifiers of an established, mature profession - with the exception, that is, of evidence of external regulation, which remains the fatal flaw that distinguishes it from established professions. A patina of professionalism has lent the profession a sheen of legitimacy which seldom stands up well to robust scrutiny, when compared to other professions, subject as they are to external scrutiny, bearing consequences for non-compliance

This fatal flaw has continued to haunt these associations since their earliest days. And no matter how hard they have tried to window-dress this lack by extolling the virtues of compensatory self-regulation, designed to shape their members' capacity to behave in a virtuous and ethical manner, it became clear that no amount of lip-service to self-regulation would stop some coaches from engaging in questionable or even corrupt practises. In the absence of such regulation or control, there was no shortage of extravagant marketing claims made by these associations, or by the less scrupulous of their members or provider partners. This marketing was directed not only towards individual coaches who were seeking a professional home, but also towards corporate and governmental institutions which were looking to grow their own internal coaching capacity to support their managers in-house. These organisations needed to feel that their internal offerings were encased in some form of protective, respectable-seeming framework, offering an objective and attached benchmark for the development of professional practice.

Parallel to the growth of these associations was the emergence of specialised training and development providers offering to skill individuals in coaching practice. Indeed, quite a number of those who headed up such training organisations were also those installing themselves in leadership roles within these newly established professional associations. These skills providers were seeking, in turn, to find means of legitimising and credentialing their training offerings. In some instances, they looked to university-based business schools for these credentialing services, but discovered that those institutions set a high bar on accreditation, discouraging them from pursuing this avenue further. Not to be thwarted by this bump in the road, these pioneers then turned to the more forgiving and permissive 'independent' professional associations, where the leaders of such entities were, in some cases, training providers in their own right. This symbiosis created a reinforcing circle that worked to the commercial benefit of the training providers while serving to polish the professional sheen of the associations. Without any form of external regulation, this reinforcing circle could proceed unhindered. The associations were, as often as not, marking their own homework, while projecting the appearance of external jurisprudence.

The social construction of celebrity coaches among the leadership

Within a wider social context in the late nineties and early noughties, where celebrity in all its forms was becoming increasingly manufactured and its creations adulated, it was not difficult for a number of these early founders to play to this zeitgeist and socially construct celebrity coach status for themselves. It is interesting to look back, now, at how various leaders of these main professional bodies currently shape their 'foundation stories,' as they reflect on their seminal part in the creation of these now impregnably successful associations. Hardly surprisingly, these foundation stories freight epic accounts of the deeds of the early heroes and founding fathers, as the myths of the founders coalesce into the formation stories of the associations themselves, stories that speak to the meeting of unconsciously desired but hitherto unserved needs of executive coaches.

For many of those involved in the start-up of these associations, we have to assume that their impulse was not one of naked profit seeking, but rather of wishing to do good work, and act in good faith, in an often-murky commercial world. In alignment with this altruistic intent, these entities, by and large, chose to adopt constitutional arrangements through vehicles such as 'limited by association companies' which constrained the leaders and executives of those associations from directly making a profit out of the association itself. Even now, if pressed on the possibility that they could exploit their positioning for commercial gain, association leaders emphasise that they have no power or control over their organisations. However, a closer inspection of this denial reveals that, by virtue of the roles and oversight such leaders occupy, they exercise 'virtual ownership' over almost all aspects of the organisation's functioning, including the allocation of funds coming in from membership, and the allocation of stipends and licences to associated training and credentialing providers.

As these associations grew in substance, they became emboldened enough to disguise the impossibility of external regulation by the substitution of that with the promotion of 'pseudo regulation,' and through the creation of a 'hyperreality' that suggested that a substantive creation had been breathed into life – as opposed to what was, in reality, closer to resembling a fragile House of Cards that could be blown over at any point by those determined enough to do the same. Yet the fact remained that too many players were invested in the manifestation of a robust profession to raise a dissenting voice.

If such voices were raised, then the messianic leaders of these associations would, on a frequent basis, underline their claims to a 'vocational' calling. by reminding all who would challenge them that they themselves were selfless volunteers, taking no profit at all in the financial sense from their leadership roles, while surrounded by a volunteer army invested with an identical missionary purpose. Indeed, even today, some such leaders are at pains to point out how they are losing professional ground and missing out on commercial gain through selflessly giving their time to the impassioned growth of their professional association.

Manufacturing the 'volunteer defence.'

In making this claim for the power of their volunteer workforce, these leaders were not exaggerating. There is little doubt that the engine that was driving the growth and consolidation of these associations arose from the efforts of volunteers, not only at the central leadership level but also regionally, and through a whole phalanx of project teams. Whilst there was no or little financial compensation for these volunteers, there existed non-transactional benefits to be had for them in occupying these roles. These benefits included the raising of their personal profile in the eyes of the membership, not least in emphasising their closeness to the associations' heroic leaders in service of making practice and regulatory breakthroughs. Such volunteers brought high levels of amateur enthusiasm to that work, which was of necessity part time.

As the associations grew in complexity and sheer scale, then the demands upon these volunteers grew increasingly weighty. While the hyperreality of the associations' marketing promises raised ever higher expectations among the membership, then very often the delivery of these promises was constrained by the skills or sheer limited availability of the volunteers themselves. Should members of the association complain about poor service, then they would almost invariably be met by the 'volunteer defence,' which parses as 'our staff and leaders are giving their time for nothing here; please bear with us; we are here for the greater good; please understand that and be patient. Be humble, just as we are.' For example, the ICF UK currently pronounce, 'The first UK ICF Board was a group of volunteers who passionately believed in the professionalisation of coaching – something we still pride ourselves on today. All our UK ICF Board members are professional coaches and work on the board as volunteers. Please feel free to contact us if we can support you in any way.' In this statement we witness the volunteer defence in a nutshell, saying we are both professionals and passionate volunteers working towards professionalisation – without dwelling on the intrinsic strains and tensions at work within this marriage of amateurism and professionalism. These are elided, and both presented as a virtue.

Is coaching intrinsically virtuous?

The virtues of professions such as medicine or law are rooted in their inherent commitment to the well-being and service of others. These occupations demand a high standard of moral conduct, as they directly impact the lives of individuals and societies. The virtuous nature of these professions can be attributed to several key factors: the pursuit of knowledge and expertise, a commitment to ethical principles, the importance of empathy and compassion, and the cultivation of trust and integrity. Both medicine and law require long-term education and continuous learning, driven by the desire to provide the best possible service to others. The devotion to acquiring knowledge and honing skills demonstrates a commitment to excellence, a virtue that is essential in these fields. By striving to deepen their expertise, professionals in medicine or law affirm their dedication to making informed and responsible decisions, placing the well-being and justice of others above personal gain.

Furthermore, virtuous professions uphold a strong commitment to ethical principles. Medical professionals, for instance, must adhere to the principles of medical ethics, such as autonomy, beneficence, non-maleficence, and justice. The ethical framework guides their decision-making process and ensures that their actions prioritize the best interests of their patients. Similarly, lawyers are bound by strict codes of professional conduct, ensuring that their representation of clients is guided by principles of fairness, justice, and the pursuit of truth. Upholding these ethical standards serves as a moral compass for professionals, ensuring that their actions align with the public good and the values of society.

Empathy and compassion form another crucial component of virtuous professions. In medicine, doctors and nurses must exhibit a deep understanding and empathy for their patients' experiences, providing not only medical treatment but also emotional support. Similarly, in law, lawyers must exhibit compassion and empathy to understand the needs and concerns of their clients and work towards their best interests. By fostering a genuine connection with those they serve, professionals in these fields establish a more holistic approach to their work, which is essential to providing effective and empathetic care.

Lastly, trust and integrity are fundamental to the virtuous nature of these professions. Doctors and lawyers are entrusted with sensitive information, and they must maintain strict confidentiality to ensure trust between themselves and their clients or patients. Additionally, acting with integrity means being honest and transparent, even in cases where difficult decisions must be made. Trust and integrity are the building blocks of a strong professional relationship, ensuring that professionals can effectively serve their clients or patients without sacrificing ethical standards.

At times these professions are referred to by those within it as a 'vocation,' or 'calling,' indicating a strong desire to engage in that particular occupation or profession. Many coaches are passionate about supporting and empowering others, and they view coaching as more than just a job or a means of earning income. They see it as a fulfilling and purpose-driven vocation, where they can make a positive impact on the lives of their clients. Like any vocation, coaching also involves a sense of responsibility towards clients, maintaining ethical standards, and continuously honing one's coaching skills.

Many coaches feel a deep sense of fulfilment and satisfaction from helping others succeed and grow, which further reinforces coaching as a vocation rather than just a profession. This sense of coaching comprising a vocation was strongly felt at the early pioneering stages of its professional development, as is often still lauded as such, despite the depredations of commercialism. For instance, you will hear coaches say, 'the moment I started to coach, I realised that this was what missing in my life. I feel so fulfilled, so like my best self, and now never want to do anything else.'

Downsides of Professionalising

History tells us that, for other areas of practice that broadly parallel coaching, such as counselling or psychological services, professionalising a field or occupation can bring several benefits, not least the conferring of legitimacy and marketability. However, there are potential dangers or challenges associated within the professionalising process. Professionalising can create barriers to entry for individuals who may have valuable skills or experience but lack formal qualifications or credentials. This can limit diversity within the profession and exclude talented individuals who could contribute positively. This phenomenon is often described within these professions as, 'pulling up the drawbridge.'

Professionalising may lead to a focus on standardisation and uniformity, potentially stifling innovation, creativity, and alternative perspectives within the field. It may prioritise conformity over diversity, resulting in limited approaches to practice. Professionalising often involves acquiring formal education, certification, or licensing, which can place a financial burden on individuals seeking to enter or advance within the profession, which may again hinder socioeconomic diversity and limit opportunities for those with limited financial resources.

The establishment of pseudo - regulatory frameworks in professionalising can potentially lead to monopolistic or overly powerful professional bodies. This can result in regulatory capture, where the interests of the profession dominate over the public interest, leading to self-serving behaviours and a lack of accountability. Professional associations or providers may be slow to adapt to societal or technological changes, causing them to lag behind emerging trends or developments in the field. This can lead to a disconnect between the profession and real-world needs or expectations. Much is made in the rhetoric of the 'gap between theory and practice,' as is the case in professional coaching. Professionalising may result in the creation of bureaucratic processes and excessive red tape within the profession. This can hinder efficiency, stifle innovation, and add administrative burdens, not least when associations such as a number of those in coaching rely on a thinly staffed volunteer force to resource the bureaucracy. These stifling processes can create rigid structures and prescribed practices, limiting the ability of professionals to adapt respond quickly to evolving needs or emerging challenges.

The professional associations may attempt to establish a monopoly or restrict competition within the profession. This could involve influencing regulations or licensing requirements to exclude or limit the entry of other professionals or competing organisations. They may also choose to cartel with other professional coaching associations. Exploitation could occur if a professional association imposes exorbitant fees for membership, certifications, or licensing. This places a financial burden on professionals and may discourage individuals from joining or advancing within the profession.

An exploitative professional association may not be transparent in its decision-making, rule-setting, or operations. This lack of transparency can lead to unfair practices, favouritism, or the exclusion of certain individuals or groups within the profession. An exploitative professional association may fail to hold its members accountable for their conduct or ethical breaches. This can undermine public trust and confidence in the profession and its practitioner. If a professional association prioritises its own interests over of the profession or the public, it may engage in self-serving behaviours. This could those involve lobbying for policies or regulations that primarily benefit the professional association itself or its leadership.

To what extent are professional coaching associations subject to these downsides of professionalisation? Depending on which association you look at, a number are exhibit some of these downsides to regulation. It can be argued that all of them are subject, to some degree to one or more of these manifestations, as they proceed through the pioneering phase towards maturity, as outlined in the later description of this trajectory.

Governance and control through 'pseudo-regulation'

Coaching associations around the world have come to realise that external regulation, and certainly global level regulation, is simply not a viable option for their field, though this realisation is rarely vocalised. When challenged, the associations protest that they are working towards unified standards of enforceable regulation, which is to some extent true, manifesting as it does such a wide range of coaching practices, methodologies, and approaches. The field of coaching is too diffuse to be effectively regulated by an external authority, who shy away from regulation conversations on these very grounds. However, these individual associations have attempted to develop strategies that compensate for this fatal flaw.

Given the absence of external regulation, the professional coaching associations are susceptible to the phenomenon of 'pseudo regulation,' which refers to the deceptive appearance or pretence of regulation within a particular profession. It occurs when a profession or occupation creates structures or mechanisms that imitate regulatory practices without adhering to the standards, accountability, or oversight typically associated with genuine regulation.

'Pseudo regulation' can take various forms, but some common characteristics may include exhibiting a lack true independence from the profession or occupation it claims to regulate. Instead of being governed by an independent association with no vested interests, the regulatory mechanisms may be controlled or heavily influenced by the practitioners themselves. Pseudo-regulation lacks proper mechanisms for addressing complaints, disciplining practitioners, or enforcing consequences for wrongdoing, operating without transparency or public accountability. The decision-making processes, rules, and regulations may be unclear, non-existent, or manipulated by the profession's elite groups or vested interests. This absence of oversight can lead to unchecked practices or behaviours within the profession.

Pseudo regulation can be problematic within coaching associations if it creates the illusion of a regulated and accountable profession while failing to protect the public interest, ensure competence, or uphold ethical standards. It can undermine public trust and confidence in professional services. Additionally, it may hinder competition, limit entry into the profession, and restrict innovation by maintaining barriers to entry and creating artificial monopolies.

Compensatory acts of pseudo-regulation include for the establishment of comprehensive certification processes, lending an aura of self-regulation and maintenance of certain standards within the field, reinforced by ostensibly robust professional codes of ethics. These codes outline the standards of behaviour, professionalism, and integrity expected from coaches. They claim to serve as a guide for ethical decision-making and provide a foundation for self-regulation within the coaching community. To compensate for the lack of external regulation, many coaching associations require coaches to engage in regular supervision and undertake continuous professional development activities.

A major weakness in the absence of regulatory association in coaching is that it provokes scepticism amongst clients and stakeholders. To counter this, coaching associations resort to strategies to highlight their supposed legitimacy and credibility. Attempts to camouflage the lack of external regulation through self-regulation, reliance on industry standards, and peer review systems is easily enough spotted by discerning clients, raising concerns regarding accountability and transparency. Without external oversight, self-regulation can be prone to biases, conflicts of interest, and a lack of checks and balances. Coaching association tend to inflate their necessity by positioning themselves as gatekeepers of ethical conduct. They create a narrative that coaching would descend into chaos and malpractice without their intervention, into the hands of the dreaded 'cowboys,' though despite pronouncements by authorative sounding leaders and advocates, coaching associations have little or no capability to safeguard practice.

The lack of external regulation paves the way for the proliferation of untrained and unqualified individuals in the coaching field, undermining the credibility and effectiveness of coaching as a profession. Coaching bodies, in an attempt to address this concern, often emphasise the importance of professional development, ongoing training, and obtaining recognised qualifications. While these measures are undoubtedly valuable, they can provide a false sense of security. Without external regulation, there is a potential for misleading claims, exaggerated credentials, or questionable business practices.

Some coaching associations may use aggressive marketing tactics to enhance their reputation and convince potential members to join them, even if their actual qualifications and claims of benefits from joining are not well-substantiated. Unethical strategies can have a significant impact on the credibility and reputation of coaching association within the industry. Some of the ways in which this impact may occur include lack of trust; reputational damage; loss of clients and members, and possible legal consequences: Unethical strategies can often have legal implications, such as fraud, misrepresentation, or violation of privacy laws. Legal action against coaching associations or coaches can further tarnish their credibility and reputation, leading to long-term damage and carry industry-wide impact: The unethical behaviour of a coaching association can cast doubt on the professionalism and ethical practices of the entire coaching industry.

It is rarely recognised that unethical strategies employed by a coaching association can create a moral and ethical dilemma for individual coaches tethered to the association. Coaches may find themselves questioning whether to continue their affiliation and potentially compromise their own values or disassociate from the coaching association, which can negatively impact their professional connections and networks.

While some association may genuinely strive for standards of excellence, others may exploit the lack of external regulation to maintain their market dominance without contributing substantively to coaching practices. By claiming exclusive access to specialised knowledge or expertise, such as competency grids for example, as a 'gold standard,' such associations attempt to establish themselves as indispensable, separating themselves from the field.

The absence of external regulation and the questionable strategies adopted by some coaching associations creates an environment conducive to mis-selling of memberships and accreditations. This mis-selling occurs when coaching association make unsupported assertions about the benefits and outcomes of being a member or obtaining specific accreditations. As a result, unsuspecting professionals invest their time, money, and trust based on these claims, only to realise later that the value and legitimacy they have been promised are not delivered.

At what point do coaching association expose themselves to legal jeopardy from their own members? As awareness grows regarding the lack of external regulation, professionals may start questioning the veracity of claims made by coaching bodies. Dissatisfied members who feel misled, inadequately supported, or that their investment has not yielded the promised results may consider legal action against these bodies. The potential for legal repercussions arises when coaching association are unable to substantiate their claims and members can prove mis-selling based on false representations. As coaching involves providing guidance and advice, coaches often find themselves in a position of trust and influence over vulnerable clients. In cases where coaching association fail to uphold ethical or professional standards, clients may take legal action against them, claiming professional misconduct, negligence, or breach of duty.

Coaching associations that have positioned themselves as authoritative entities may face significant legal scrutiny if their certifications, memberships, or endorsements are perceived as misleading or lacking substance. Engaging in deceptive practices or providing inadequate supervision could lead to allegations of fraudulent misrepresentation and miss-selling, leading to potential lawsuits. Indeed, there is evidence that several coaching associations are not slow to mobilise expert – and expensive – legal counsel should they fear themselves to be under challenge from members who ask questions of their claims to ethical and professional leadership behaviour.

The creation of hyperreality through marketing hype

Pseudo-regulation can be reinforced by the creation of 'hyperreality' in coaching associations' marketing. This refers to the use of exaggerated or idealised representations of coaching services and outcomes for promotional purposes. It involves creating a perception of coaching that may not necessarily reflect the actual experiences or results. It is important to consider the potential impacts and ethical implications of hyperreality in coaching association marketing. These marketing strategies often involve creating an illusion of exclusivity, prestige, and specialised knowledge that can only be accessed through their certifications or memberships. Such tactics may lead individuals seeking coaching services to believe that these association possess superior expertise and qualifications which are more apparent than real.

When coaching associations employ hyperreality in their marketing, they often do so through the medium of eye-catching graphics and photos depicting a perfected image of coaching association, without a single word of the downsides of joining such an organisation, creating unrealistic expectations among potential members. They may anticipate extraordinary results or transformations that are not be achievable in reality, resulting in disappointment and a loss of trust in the coaching association. Hyperreality raises ethical concerns related to honesty and transparency in marketing. If coaching associations exaggerate or misrepresent the benefits or effectiveness of coaching, they can be viewed as deceptive or manipulative. Hyperreality can overshadow the real value and genuine outcomes that coaching can provide. By focusing on exaggerated representations, coaching associations may detract from the actual benefits and positive impacts that coaching can have on individuals and organisations.

Power, control and 'virtual ownership' among coaching associations

When coaching association leaders are pressed as to the ownership of their associations, they are often quick to point out that this is not they who are the 'owners.' Rather, they point to the fact that the majority of such associations, with the exception of the US based ICF, (International Coaching Federation) are 'companies limited by association,' registered in UK. While it may well be true that the designated directors of such entities do not have formal ownership in a structural sense, there is evidence that these leaders may exert 'virtual ownership.'

To understand the concept of 'virtual ownership,' it is crucial to recognise that 'ownership' does not always require legal and financial ownership. Virtual ownership refers to the ability to exercise control and influence over an organisation or entity without possessing traditional ownership rights. It can manifest through various means, including leadership authority, strategic decision-making, and regulatory practices.

In the case of professional coaching bodies, their leaders often function as stewards, governing and steering the organisation towards its goals and objectives. While they may not have ownership stakes, they hold substantial power in shaping the direction and functioning of these bodies. Through their roles, they can establish policies, frameworks, and guidelines that govern the coaching industry. One way in which professional coaching associations exert virtual ownership is through the creation and enforcement of standards and regulations. These associations set criteria for coaching practices within their own organisations, seeking to ensure that coaches meet specific qualifications and adhere to defined ethical guidelines. By establishing and claiming to maintain such standards, coaching associations influence the entire industry and indirectly influence which coaches are considered legitimate and trustworthy.

Furthermore, through their leadership positions, these associations have the power to influence coaching education and training programs. They often collaborate with educational institutions to develop curriculum guidelines and establish accreditation processes for coach training. Consequently, they control the quality and content of coaching education, giving them significant influence over the knowledge and skills coaches acquire.

Professional coaching associations also assert virtual ownership by developing and implementing professional codes of conduct. These codes serve as the guiding principles for coaches' professional behaviour, emphasising ethical conduct, confidentiality, client welfare, and conflict resolution. By setting these standards, coaching associations shape the coaching profession's ethical landscape, thereby exerting control and influence over coaches' actions.

Moreover, these associations often act as central hubs for coach networking, continuing education, and career development. They provide platforms for coaches to connect, exchange knowledge, and enhance their skills. By organising events, conferences, and workshops, professional coaching associations create opportunities for coaches to learn and develop professionally, exerting virtual ownership over the coaching community, especially where association leaders are showcased at such events.

A major concern in contexts where leaders exert high control, despite not owning the associations they run, is the absence of sufficient accountability. Without formal ownership, leaders may feel less obliged to answer to others or justify their decisions. The lack of clear ownership can lead to an unchecked exercise of authority, potentially detaching the leaders from the body's purpose and the interests of its members. Virtual ownership exercised through excessive control can lead to a reduction in diversity and instead mean a concentration of power within professional coaching bodies. When leaders monopolise decision-making processes and hold considerable control, they may inadvertently hinder the representation of diverse voices and perspectives within the organisation. This can limit innovation, stifle progress, and push forward an agenda that may not necessarily align with the broader interests of the coaching community.

The virtual ownership phenomenon can impede professional development within coaching bodies. Leaders who tightly control these associations may prioritise their personal choices for CPD rather than fostering an environment that encourages continual learning and growth across a wide range of offerings. This limitation negatively impacts the overall quality and effectiveness of coaching practices as coaching associations with restricted professional development opportunities struggle to keep up with industry advancements.

The concept of virtual ownership can blur the lines between the leaders' interests and the objectives of the professional coaching associations they oversee. High control placed in the hands of leaders who are not formally recognised as owners can result in conflicts of interest, leading to decisions that may primarily serve personal motivations rather than the collective well-being of the coaching profession. Such conflicts can undermine the credibility of coaching associations and erode the trust of coaches and the wider community.

One defence their influence commonly given by leaders exerting virtual ownership is the use of volunteers within these bodies. By associating volunteerism with virtuous intentions, leaders aim to deflect criticism regarding their possible high control or perhaps less than virtuous intentions. However, declaring that all volunteers are virtuous fails to acknowledge the potential for abuse of power or personal agendas. This defence may serve to create a false perception of virtue, aligned with a an emphasis on positivity that infuses the associations, which further obstructs a thorough examination of the leaders' actions and intentions.

The playing out of neo-feudalism among coaching associations

Among commentators on the contemporary professional scene, there is a growing concern that certain aspects of the socio-economic system resemble elements of a neo-feudalistic structure. While the term "neo-feudalism" may seem antiquated and disconnected from our modern reality, its relevance lies in its ability to shed light on the challenges posed by the professionalisation ecosystem.

One of the core pillars of feudalism was the concentration of power in the hands of a select few. Similarly, in the professionalisation ecosystem, power and influence often gravitate towards large corporations, major industry players, and influential individuals. This concentration of power results in limited access and opportunities for those outside these privileged circles, mirroring the feudalistic hierarchy that restricted opportunities for the majority.

Neo-feudalism perpetuates wealth disparities between those at the top and those left at the bottom, further stressing the growing socio-economic divide. In the professionalisation ecosystem, this translates into wealth asymmetries between high-ranking professionals and the rest of the workforce. This alarming trend threatens social cohesion and perpetuates systemic inequality. Feudal societies were characterised by a lack of upward social mobility, defining societal roles based on inherited positions rather than individual talent or merit. Traces of this phenomenon can be seen in the professionalisation ecosystem, where factors like nepotism, privilege, and occasional disregard for qualifications impede equitable opportunities for advancement. This undermines a meritocratic approach, limiting social mobility and stifling innovative potential within our diverse society.

Feudal subjects had limited autonomy and agency over their lives, as their choices and actions were constrained by their fiefdoms. In the professionalisation ecosystem, individuals may find their autonomy curtailed due to contractual obligations, power imbalances, and limited bargaining power. Moreover, the rise of automation and the potential displacement of human workers adds an additional layer of control, further questioning the extent of individual agency within this system.

Bob Garvey, in 'Neofeudalism and surveillance in coaching supervision and mentoring?' (Garvey, 2014) argues persuasively for the role supervision plays in imposing neo feudal practices upon the coaching ecosystem. He states '(Neo-feudalism) is driven by rules and an assumption of compliance and therefore, control. Arguably the modern workplace seeks control through surveillance processes to extract compliance - i.e., appraisal and PDRs, performance management, 360° feedback and perhaps coaching (Nielsen & Nørreklit, 2009). Professional associations claim that supervision, as one of their requirements for accreditation, reassures potential clients or sponsors and ensures quality control. Is this a form of neofeudalistic surveillance? With coaching and mentoring's roots in person centred humanism, is there a paradox? If so, how can we move forward?'

Just as Garvey would argue for the role that supervision plays in the social construction of neofeudalism; so, too, could one argue that accreditation - as opposed to wider credentialing - plays a powerful reinforcing role in the creation of the professionalising discourse. Accreditation is not neutral in this discourse of ownership and control of the profession, where patterns of reinforcement are in play between the original establishment of the professional body; the laying down of governance ordinances and protocols; the setting of standards; the creation of competency models: the outlining of accreditation criteria; the lining up of providers of learning products that align with those criteria, followed by the skilling up a cadre of assessors to qualify candidates as they seek to pass muster. This process of assessing coaches is not a one-off act but continues for periodic renewal of accreditation thereafter. The requirement for supervision places a further layer of assessment and surveillance on the practitioner.

This interlocking system of member capture would be significantly weakened if the candidates chose not to engage with the accreditation process. Once this accreditation step is taken, then fallacious 'sunk cost' arguments can pressure the candidate to financially invest further in this system, thus strengthening their psychological contract, even if they harbour some background reservations regarding the efficacy of system, which can grow, the deeper they enter in.

Garvey argues that 'With coaching and mentoring's roots in person-centered humanism, is there a paradox?' There could well be, but only if you subscribe to the assumption that coaching needs to continue to valorise its Rogerian roots. If, on the other hand, the coach is accepting of the tenets of managerialism and control, then the idea of joining a body that is heavily vested in the same would not be at all dissonant. In fact it would be accepted as a normal characteristic of doing business.

Brand building around celebrity coaches' personas.

Across professional coaching associations, the trend towards them being led by or pairing with charismatic celebrity coaches has become increasingly common. As these 'celebrity coaches' gain fame and recognition through their successful careers, research claims and subsequent media exposure, coaching associations attempt to leverage their influence by claiming affiliation with these celebrities in a mutually reinforcing circle.

First and foremost, a major concern regarding this affiliation is that charisma alone does not guarantee coaching effectiveness or professional expertise. While these celebrities may possess magnetic personalities and impressive track records, their public image and appeal should not overshadow the experience and qualifications required for effective coaching. Another crucial reason for caution is the potential inconsistency between a celebrity coach's brand persona and a coaching associations values or goals. Celebrity coaches are not always aligned with the methodologies, approaches, or ethics that a coaching association may hold dear. By blindly associating with charismatic coaches, coaching associations risk diluting their own identity and damaging their reputation.

The reliance on celebrity coaches can create an overdependence on individuals rather than building a robust coaching institution. Should the celebrity coach retire, change careers, or even face public scandal, the coaching company's reputation would be significantly affected. These dynamics are particularly acute when the celebrity is the one of the founders of the association – or claims to be - which is often the case.

Navigating the 'founder's dilemma.'

When coaching companies rigidly adhere to a celebrity founder's playbook, they limit the possibility of innovation and adaptability. If coaching associations are bound to replicating a particular framework, they might fail to address the diverse range of challenges and developmental needs that their members present. Consequently, a narrower range of coaching methods might exclude potential members who do not connect with or find value in the founder's approach.

Another potential danger of coaching companies that strictly adhere to the founder's methods is the risk of a seeming to generate a cult-like following. Well-known coaches often develop cults of personality around themselves, attracting a dedicated group of followers who adopt their methods and beliefs unquestioningly. This blind adherence to a single approach can hinder critical thinking and personal growth. Association members may become reliant on the celebrity coach's methods without exploring alternative perspectives or approaches to their problems. This dependency on a specific method deprives individuals of the opportunity to develop their own problem-solving skills and self-reliance, which are fundamental aspects of personal development.

Moreover, an uncritical acceptance of the founder's methods can lead to a lack of scientific rigour and evidence-based practice within coaching companies. Sometimes, coaching approaches are based purely on the founder's personal experiences or anecdotes, devoid of any empirical evidence or validated research. This absence of robust empirical grounding limits the credibility and efficacy of coaching interventions. Without a commitment to evidence-based practice, coaching companies risk falling into pseudoscience or unverified claims, potentially harming clients who rely on their services for meaningful change.

Creating a 'messiah complex' to cultivate cult-like cultures

A messiah complex is characterised by a belief in one's exceptionalism, omniscience, and a desire to impose their views upon others. This can result in ethical transgressions, such as manipulation, coercion, or the promotion of unhealthy dependencies. Celebrity coaches tend to cultivate a strong personal brand and develop a devoted following, creating an unhealthy power dynamic and blind adherence to the coach's methods, even if they may not be suitable or evidence based. People influenced by the 'messiah complex' may lack critical thinking and exhibit an over-reliance on the leader's teachings, posing ethical concerns. Coaches who believe they possess all the answers may neglect to consider the specific needs, values, and circumstances of their clients, leading to a one-size-fits-all approach that may not yield the desired outcomes.

This often arises from an imbalance of power, with the founder assuming an elevated, almost god-like position, while members perceive themselves as being incapable without their leader's intervention. Messiahs may be so consumed by their perceived greatness that they become resistant to external feedback and fail to recognise their own flaws and limitations. Coaching approaches, philosophies and advice may become tainted, losing their authenticity and objectivity. These celebrity leaders, driven by their personal beliefs and ideals, may leverage their followers' vulnerabilities and insecurities to solidify their influence and power. It can also attract vulnerable individuals seeking answers and guidance. This creates an environment conducive to manipulation, as their vulnerability makes them more susceptible to exploitation. Such manipulation can lead to the exploitation of associations as they become entangled in a cycle of emotional dependence on the leader's validation and guidance.

The 'accreditation' inflection point

A collective inflection point on the maturity curve of these associations occurred when each of them, across adjacent timelines, began to develop instruments and tools for accreditation and credentialing. In the eyes of both individual members and of corporate customers. accreditation was to become a major plank in the consolidation of these associations in the eyes of business as viable commercial enterprises. In the then contemporary managerial world, competency grids were in the zeitgeist, and for many performance coaches they were at the heart of their client's developmental practice. It is hardly surprising, therefore, that the coaches to these corporate clientele would extol the virtues of applying equivalent competency technologies within their own professional structures. The coaching associations embarked on an arms race regarding the superiority of their respective accreditation offerings, some claiming that theirs were the gold standard, others speaking to the research robustness of their competency offering.

The imitating of each other's grids was rife, as credentialing contagion spread. The phenomenon of 'mimetic isomorphism' was rife, where it becomes almost impossible to copy the moves your competitors make, even if these leaves products indistinguishable one from another. Bragging about the superiority of one's offering was to display 'the vanity of small differences.' It could be claimed that with the hegemony of accreditation on the coaching landscape came the gradual displacement of the emancipatory impulse that had inflected the early birthing of these associations, which was being slowly but surely driven out by the imperative to demonstrate superiority. At this point the dominance of competency grids marked an inflection point in the transition of coaching association development from its initial pioneering phase towards a relentless systematisation phase.

The tension between those driving the embedding of managerialist competency measures, and those resisting the atomising of holistic, values-centred coaching practice is still alive today, but for many reasons attempts at reversing the competency approach has proven difficult to executive within the policies and practices of the professional associations. This implacability is explicable through the extent to which sunk-cost mentality was in play among so many of the salient stakeholders, not least among those who had strived to gain competency-based accreditations, reinforced by the voice of accreditation providers who were deeply invested in selling and 'improving' their distinctive brands.

With this arrival of systematised credentialing, it became apparent that coaches - whom at an earlier time had embraced the emancipatory principle that 'coaching is for all, and can be practised by all,' - once they had put themselves through an accreditation regimen - found themselves reassessing their allegiance to their original liberating instincts. At that point of damascene conversion, many of these earlier evangelicals became firm advocates not only for the credentials that they had painstakingly gained, at no small expense, but also began to express fealty towards the issuing body that was now formally endorsing their professionalism. At one point during this conversion process, a critical mass of such converts was heard to declare that there should be a 'pulling up of the drawbridge' among the professional associations, suggesting that only those who have passed muster through the credentialing rings and hoops would be worthy of credible and ethical practises.

Pulling up the drawbridge on the emancipatory impulse.

This member-driven cry to 'pull up the drawbridge' marked an important fork in the road for the associations, where performative professionalism gradually displaced the emphasis on coaching as a virtuous practice that could be for the benefit of all. This displacement of the altruistic impulse was reinforced by the activities of corporate coaching commissioners who, together with their acolytes in procurement and HR, deeply seated as they were in managerial practice, were keen to find a way to somehow differentiate the market pool that they were purchasing from. These consumers needed to be able to tell the difference between 'a good 'un and a bad 'un,' and to defend their choice through the application of an apparently robust benchmark process.

Coaches who were once ardently opposed to accreditation on emancipatory grounds, once they themselves become accredited now face a disconcerting question: do they seek to pull up the drawbridge on the principle that says everyone is welcome? Accreditation provides coaches with a recognised status and a sense of belonging to an elite group of professionals. However, this newfound status can inadvertently lead to a sense of exclusivity, tempting certified coaches to distance themselves from the ideology that once drove their advocacy for inclusion of all who wish to join the coaching community on emancipatory grounds in the first place. The allure of this exclusivity creates a risk that they will neglect the potential transformative power coaching holds for all individuals, not just those who can afford it or are prepared to put in the time and slog that accreditation demands.

Coaches who were initially driven by the goal of challenging societal norms and promoting critical thinking may gradually lose their passion for challenging the status quo as they embrace accreditation. The validation and acceptance that come with accreditation can inadvertently make coaches more susceptible to conformity, leading them to shy away from the challenging nature of emancipatory coaching. Consequently, they may refrain from provoking critical thoughts and behaviours that are necessary to challenge oppressive systems in the first place.

For a number of coaches, the act of embracing accreditation can dilute the potency of their previous emancipatory based approaches. They know that the broad standardisations imposed by accreditation association may limit the freedom to tailor coaching sessions to individual needs, yet they are fearful of transgressing the rules and practices installed by their accreditation training, and be judged for doing the same through supervision, adverse client feedback, or judgemental licence renewal processes. This fear of transgression might drive coaches to abandon their commitment to an emancipatory approach to coaching, opting for conformity with the standard practices instead. This dilution risks eroding the transformative potential of coaching and suppressing the very principles that led these coaches to advocate for emancipatory practices in the first place.

Accreditation provides coaches with a tangible acknowledgment of their expertise within the field. This validation can unconsciously foster a sense of self-importance, inadvertently leading some accredited coaches to believe that their expertise is superior to that of non-accredited coaches. This perception can result in a desire to distance themselves from their previously held emancipatory principles, as they may perceive the practices of non-accredited coaches as less legitimate or effective. Consequently, the very principles that encouraged their initial opposition to accreditation might be dismissed as they seek to establish their authority and expertise within the coaching community, aligning with the orthodoxy of practice leaders.

As coaches become accredited, opportunities for financial gain often increase. With the growth of the coaching industry, coaches are presented with lucrative prospects and potential financial rewards. In such circumstances, there is a likelihood that some coaches may prioritise financial gains over the ethical responsibilities they once held dear. This shift in focus may result in their abandonment of their coaching clients who lack the means to afford their services, thus perpetuating inequalities rather than striving for emancipation.

Accreditation drives elitism through desensitisation.

Coaches who previously decried the accreditation process as an unnecessary barrier may start embracing it as a sign of professional legitimacy. While it is not fair to label all accredited coaches as 'sell-outs,' some may unintentionally undermine the values they once championed. This needs to be understood as a gradual immersion in the 'boiled frog syndrome,' where the demise of something that is treasured is eroded without noticing the gradual descent. The normalisation of elitism occurs when individuals become accustomed to the privileges associated with a certain status or credential. Coaches who were initially concerned about associations manipulating accreditation as a tool for exclusion may gradually come to view it as a natural and irreversible characteristic of the coaching profession. This normalisation can result in the perpetuation of exclusive practices and the exclusion of coaches who do not possess a specific certification or accreditation.

Desensitisation refers to the gradual numbing of sensitivity towards the negative consequences of elitism. As coaches become integrated into the accredited coaching community, they may develop a diminished awareness or concern for the potential harm imposed on non-accredited individuals. This desensitisation can blind them to the barriers they once fought against, inadvertently adopting 'one-up' positioning towards less qualified coaches, exploiting those who feel some inferiority, to the point of openly or covertly discouraging them from climbing the ladder that would bring then to parity with themselves. If coaches who were initially opposed to coaching accreditation progressively accept it as an unquestionable requirement, the risk of perpetuating elitism within the coaching profession becomes a grave concern. The potential consequences include limited access to coaching for marginalised individuals, stifling of diverse perspectives, erosion of social justice efforts, and an entrenchment of power dynamics between accredited and non-accredited coaches.

This is not to suggest that the associations' marketing rhetoric extolling virtue and ethical practice had disappeared. This remained sacrosanct, most certainly at the rhetorical level. What was sacrificed by several of the associations was the notion that 'coaching was for all, provided by a wide diversity of practitioners;' and in the following through of that belief effectively excluding those who arguably most needed coaching but could least afford it. Whether intended or not, this meant a narrowing of the diversity of practitioners, conventionally qualified or not.

As the bodies grew increasingly competitive one with another, so too did the need for each of them to be pitching eye-catching product offerings which would separate them from the herd. This need to be seen to be standing on the cutting edge of innovation drove the associations towards a marketing imperative for continuous novelty, an impulse which, neatly, coincided with the motivation of many individual coaches to be collecting as many 'badges' as possible. Accredited providers of training and outsourced accreditation services to the associations were not slow to feed this appetite for newness. This critical mass behind innovation was to put the premium on shiny new product lines over established practices that had as their basis deeper principles of practice that had stood the test of time.

A paradox in all of this might be that while each of the various accreditation regimes emphasised the need for 'reflective practice' as a core competency on their assessment grids - in many ways this encouragement of deep reflective practice was being driven out by this tsunami of innovation. Indeed, this tendency towards the boxing up and breaking down of new products into easily digestible bite-sized chunks was even being applied to reflective practices, where products such as mindfulness could be commoditised and served up on screens in bite-sized chunks.

Espousing ethical codes as a proxy for external regulation.

Faced with the impossibility of external, enforceable regulation, reinforced by robust penalties, the associations deployed a variety of displacement activities that attempted to compensate for this lack. One tactic was to amplify their espoused reverence for ethical principles, which became central to the rhetorical pronouncements of these associations. So insistent was this need for ethical performativity that in 2016, the majority of these associations (but not the major player from the USA, the ICF) came together to construct, to great fanfare, a 'global code of ethics' (GCoE) that they insisted would be observed across the globe. While it was initially suggested that the signatories to this code would have the power to hold each other accountable for ethical misconduct, this obligation has now been removed.

It could be claimed that associations are now at the point where the GCoE is more honoured in the breach than in the observance, even though each new lay member joining one of the signature associations is required to tick a box on their application form that says they comply with the GCoEs, without their compliance being tested in any way before the application is accepted. Given this requirement to sign off on this code, there is no real scrutiny or face to face exploration of what this might mean for that member should a complaint be registered by one of their clients. This ethical sign-off would seem to act more for the protection of the association rather than the individual. A further ethical lapse is the failure to ask new members to give 'informed consent' at the point of purchase, a consent that would spell out potential downsides of joining an association, or of pursuing one of their accreditations, including make them aware of the true costs of pursuing the same – and a realistic view of how their marketability would be elevated, or not, as a result of gaining the credential.

Should a member voice a dissenting note regarding their association's practices or policies, or question the activities of the leadership group, there is scant evidence of constitutional processes that would allow them to register a complaint, such as whistle-blowing processes. On the contrary, within some associations there is substantive evidence of there being very real consequences attendant on members pushing back against the ministrations and activities of the executives, such as the threat of exclusion, or even following through on that to the point of expulsion. In most instances, the dissident member is worn down by a conspiracy of silence and unresponsiveness to their challenges that eventually wears down their resistance. Given the severity of possible recriminations against members in the face of alleged ethical violations, it may come as some surprise that there is no commensurate code of conduct that would apply to executives and officers of most of these coaching associations, should they transgress their own codes. This is a curious emission, given the sanctimonious nature of many of their pronouncements directed at their members.

'Content' providers roles in the accreditation eco-system.

The mainstream coaching associations did not have capacity – or choose not to have the capacity to – develop and deliver to the various trainings allegedly necessary for achieving necessary competency – therefore a wide array of coaching skills providers burgeoned in line with the legitimising of coaching associations. Business Schools were not immune in their seeking provider accreditation from coaching associations; nor to endorsing independent providers. Businesses such as the Academy of Executive Coaching in the UK grew their Unique Selling Point by providing generic coach training which aimed to unify range of differing but similar accreditation requirements of the competing associations. Indeed, the founder of the AoEC was President of EMCC UK when he developed this one-programme-fits all associations assessment criteria strategy. This universal offering gave rise to questions of conflict of interest at the time, through the conflation of an individual holding major leadership roles both in an association while leading one of its major suppliers, but that conflict was never openly addressed.

The Academy of Executive Coaching (AoEC) claim on their website that, 'a reported 83% of coaching clients ... expect... a credential from their coach practitioner.' Yet in a recent AoEC blog, a serving Director of a UK professional body states, 'there is still a lack of demand from purchasers of executive coaching services for accreditation.' The interplay between supply push and demand pull continues to fluctuate to the present day.

For those working as internal coaches, in organisational contexts such as Higher Education or NHS, coaches are encouraged to credential- up, but this is rarely compulsory. There are examples of public bodies and business schools partnering with professional bodies, to provide clunky sounding appellations such as the "EMCC EQA Bespoke Practitioner Mentoring Programme with EIA Professional Designation' fast tracking programme, which is available through the NHS, and developed and provisioned in part by a business school. Such gnomic acronyms are increasingly common on the credential landscape, and while their efficacy might be transparent to their designers, these are hardly likely to be easily understood by prospective clients who stand outside the systems and the mindsets that give rise to them in the first place.

Countering potential newbies objections to the accreditation sales pitch

In the event of a potential member respond to the pitch of a prospective professional coaching association with questions regarding the solidity of the underpinnings of this system, then they are reassured that the client requirement for accreditation is growing; that membership is growing, and they are often congratulated for choosing the best in class ('go to') professional body. If the potential customer asks whether they might be subject to regulation should they transgress the rules, they are reminded that, in their application form, that they have to sign up to a code of conduct, and that disciplinary processes are in place, should they transgress.

Should they ask if the body is answerable to external regulation, then they will be assured that self-regulation works well, as the executive and their officers are ethical citizens who act in good faith. If they pursue this line of questioning, they will be reminded that external regulation across the associations has been explored in the past, has proved problematic, but has not been dropped as an idea altogether. Questioning members will be reminded by the executive that coaching is, 'after all a new profession that is still shaking down ... and that you, as a member, are a part of that maturation process.' Once the member has made a purchase choice, then they could well be persuaded, and persuade themselves, that 'their' body is legitimate and ethical. The member is very rarely given any discomfiting news about the organisation, even when there is evidence of subterranean internal crises of purpose, of leadership or of governance. Instead, only positively crafted infomercials of expansion and breakthroughs in service offerings break to the surface.

Not only are members encouraged to buy into the conceit that their body is the best-in -class, highly ethical, and bent on societal improvement. They are also encouraged to volunteer and become an intrinsic part of 'ever upward, ever onward' professionalisation process. They are asked, 'why not join our executive to exert even more leverage on enhancement of standards and practice?' The not-so-subtle subtext is that exposure in an executive role will not only widen your network and enhance your credentials in the present. I you look at the LinkedIn profiles of past executive officers of any of the coaching bodies, then you will more than likely find that, on their profile, many of them rank their historical office, honorific and length of of service in their professional association highly.. For several such individuals, their status in their professional body entry nests neatly alongside a cataloguing of their company's coach training provision, supervision offering, and of their adjacent publications, some of which might be published by their affiliated association.

Coaching commissioners legitimise accreditation over mere membership.

Coaching commissioners, who are responsible for selecting coaching providers for their organisations, may, in their specifications, require bidders to demonstrate accreditation by a coaching provider. In the eyes of the commissioners, accreditation is a recognised and formal validation process that assesses the quality and standards of professional providers. It provides assurance to commissioners that the selected providers meet certain criteria and adhere to best practices. It is understandable then that commissioners would ask the same for coaching as they would for the more recognised professions such as engineering or HR. They prioritise accreditation as it serves as a proxy for quality assurance, indicating that the coaching provider has met specific standards set forth by the accrediting association. It assures coaching commissioners that the provider has undergone a rigorous assessment and has demonstrated competence in delivering coaching services in adherence to professional standards and ethics codes. This helps protect the interests of clients and ensures a professional coaching relationship. Accreditation typically involves a review of coaching methodologies, tools, and techniques used by the provider. This ensures that the coaching approach is consistent and effective in achieving the desired outcomes for clients.

Commissioners may prefer accredited providers because they have confidence in the coaching methods employed, as accreditation serves as a risk management tool for coaching commissioners. By selecting accredited providers, commissioners mitigate the potential risks associated with ineffective coaching, unethical practices, or subpar results. It provides a level of accountability and reduces the likelihood of negative outcomes for the commissioners themselves. 'No one ever got fired for hiring McKinsey.' While accreditation may not be the sole criterion for selecting coaching providers, it can be a valuable factor considered by coaching commissioners, especially those from the procurement function who may be relatively unschooled in assessing coach provision.

Some coaching commissioners may prioritise working with coaching providers that have recognised accreditations because it adds credibility to the coaching process. Accreditation by reputable coaching associations or associations can enhance the reputation and trustworthiness of the coaching provider, increasing their appeal in the selection process – and furthermore it justifies using coaching in the first place, thus deflecting sceptical executives who may well question why their company should ever commission coaching interventions in the first place.

Accreditation is generally considered more important than mere membership of a coaching association when coaching commissioners are selecting a coach. While membership in a coaching association indicates affiliation with a professional organisation, accreditation signifies that the coach has met specific criteria and standards set forth by an accrediting association. Accreditation carries more weight for as it appears to represent a comprehensive evaluation of a coach's qualifications, skills, experience, and adherence to professional standards. This assessment process goes beyond basic membership requirements and provides a more thorough validation of a coach's competence. Accreditation demonstrates that the coach has undergone a rigorous evaluation process and has met specific benchmarks.

Accrediting associations generally have a code of ethics that all coaches must ostensibly uphold – though this is rarely checked. This means that member coaches are expected to follow ethical guidelines and conduct themselves in an appropriate and professional manner. This aspect is crucial for coaching commissioners who want to ensure that coaches working with their organisation align with ethical principles.

Accreditation on top of mere membership is perceived by the client to reinforce this commitment to ethical practice, protecting clients' interests by providing a further layer of accountability. Accredited coaches are bound by the standards and practices set by the accrediting association as judged by a competency grid, and clients can have confidence that the coach will act in their best interests. Accreditation adds credibility and trustworthiness to the coaching profession. While membership of a coaching association can still be valuable, accreditation offers a more concrete and comprehensive evaluation of a coach's qualifications. It provides a veneer of assurance, of quality, professionalism, and adherence to recognised standards, making it a stronger indicator for coaching commissioners when selecting a coach.

Niche coaching associations conforming to accreditation tropes

Many self- proclaimed niche or 'alternative' coaching enterprises – whilst they claim to abjure the reductionist, one-size-fits-all, competency-based approaches of the mainstream coaching associations – have, over time, gone on to develop their own versions of accreditation that coaches may wish to display on their marketing materials. Simon Western's systemically based Analytic Network Coaching company now offers an 'advanced diploma course,' and has also adopted wholesale the GCoE, without becoming a signatory. David Drake's narrative coaching company 'Moment Institute' offers a variety of levels of accreditation and mastery. Otto Sharmer's 'Theory U' practice offers a sophisticated range of accreditation, some of which build towards ICF accreditation. These three businesses main marketing efforts aim at individual coaches who serve corporate or organisation markets, or directly to the corporates themselves.

Then there is the myriad of 'positive psychology' and NLP based coaching providers, whose main market is in the provision of individual 'life coach' market. Some of their products, which began as outliers, are now bleeding into mainstream professional provision, through delivery of wellness programmes and the likes.

Radical networks cannot resist the solidifying 'Institute' signifier.

It seems paradoxical that self-proclaimed alternative, radical networks, built around the charisma and teachers and founders, should resort to the signifier 'Institute,' yet they do. The Moment Institute, the Ecoleadership Institute, the Presencing Institute. The semiotics of this term seem pretty obvious, claiming maturity and permanence in a world in flux, separating them from evanescent networks that bloom and die like desert flowers.

Meanwhile, patrician elders have evolved from their earlier commercial incarnations towards the creation of Institutes also, such as Peter Hawkin's creation of his 'Global Team Coaching Institute' in partnership with old business rivals.

Business executives and association leaders in common cause.

A growing marketing trend among coaching associations concerns the promotion and publication of the relationship between executive coaching clients and their coaches. This promotion of the partnership between executive clients and their coaches is effected through seminars, conferences and publications, and often reinforced by the marketing materials of coaching associations. In all of this, coaches valorise their prestigious clients, while at the same time elevating themselves, by association, to a similar status and profile, basking in the reflected glory that client affirmation of the coaches role in a business transformation provides. If one doubts this claim, then witness how many coaches on LinkedIn or on their websites seek to differentiate themselves by claiming that they principally (or exclusively!) work at 'CEO or C-suite level.'

This emphasis on portraying clients as commercial 'heroes' can create an environment where coaches are more focused on the promotion and glorification of their clients, as much as they are on fostering client's genuine personal growth, and possibly compromising, or undermining the integrity of their coaching in the process. As coaches increasingly valorise their clients as heroes, the clients become recipients of adulation and affirmation. This projection may well reduce the client's ability to engage in an open and honest coaching relationship, potentially perpetuating the coaching relationship solely for validation and shared market promotion rather than development.

By selectively highlighting the heroic successes and achievements of their clients, coaches may inadvertently ignore the flaws and vulnerabilities that make individuals human. This obsession with heroism and celebrity may disregard the importance of embracing failures and addressing personal challenges, which are essential aspects of growth, though the clients 'journey' from failure or an impasse to glorious breakthrough may well be alluded to. As coaches continue to valorise their clients as heroes, an unrealistic expectation is created for both parties involved. Clients may feel pressured to maintain an image of greatness and heroism, fearing the consequences of declaring vulnerability and shortcomings. On the other hand, coaches themselves may succumb to the hubristic desire for hero-like status, fuelled by this collusion between executives and coaching association leaders.

The valorisation of clients as heroes and the subsequent desire of coaches to be seen as coaching heroes or 'rock stars,' they unintentionally reinforce the idea of dependency and subservience. By positioning themselves as the saviours or the guides, coaches inadvertently undermine the autonomy and agency of their clients. This can lead to leaders becoming reliant on their coaches rather than developing their own problem-solving skills, hindering their growth and development in the longer run.

This can create an environment where coaches prioritise their own success rather than the needs of their clients. As a result, the coaching relationship becomes skewed, and the true purpose of coaching – facilitating growth and development – is compromised. Coaches may even, inadvertently, blur boundaries and engage in behaviours that breach ethical standards, ranging from inappropriate relationships to exploiting clients for personal gain or recognition, which undermines the integrity of the coaching profession.

When the culture around executive coaching becomes synonymous with an element of reciprocal hero worship, then it risks being seen as a superficial, self-promoting industry rather than a legitimate profession aimed at facilitating growth and development. This not only undermines the value of coaching but also makes it difficult for leaders to access authentic and effective coaching support when it is truly needed. CEOs keenly observe the habits and choices of their peers. As a result, they may well seek to gain the services of a celebrity coach who works for a fellow CEO, viewing that capture as the gaining of some kind of trophy, without fully engaging with the demands for personal scrutiny that coaching ostensibly requires.

The narrative of the heroic leader can erode humility, a vital quality for effective leadership. When executives are consistently valorised as heroes by their coaches, they might become less receptive to feedback, less likely to seek input from their teams, and more resistant to admitting mistakes or weaknesses. This erosion of humility can impede personal growth and hinder a leader's ability to establish trusting relationships with colleagues. Ultimately, the success of an organisation depends on the collective effort of a team, not solely on the individual leader.

When executive coaching becomes centred around idolising the client, it can undermine the principle of accountability. The client's actions and decisions may face less critical evaluation, even if they are detrimental to the organisation or its employees. Coaches, who are supposed to guide and challenge their clients, may hesitate to confront them regarding questionable choices or ethics for fear of seeming unsupportive. This lack of accountability fosters an environment where leaders may become complacent, increasing the risk of poor decision-making and potential harm to stakeholders.

When executive coaching becomes synonymous with hero worship, it risks being seen as a superficial, self-promoting industry rather than a legitimate profession aimed at facilitating growth and development. Coaching associations fit into this picture in the sense that the high-profile celebrity coaches attached to coaching associations are often the actors who engage in the elevation of their clients' heroic achievements, and along the way enjoy the reflected glory. Coaching bodies are also increasingly differentiating their offerings between individual and corporate service streams. Attachment to a prominent client within such a corporate client will surely drive the take-up their product offerings within that client system.

Giving prominence to the myth of the hero-leader can also play to elevation of the leaders of coaching associations as being heroes in their own right, as worthy of an unchallenged dependence as that accorded to industry leaders. In the same way – given their self-styled titles such as CEO, President, VP, etc, - they socially construct their profile and legitimacy as able business leaders in the eyes of their followers. Beyond the coaching association they lead, they are often not shy to promote themselves through drawing attention to prestigious roles and job titles within that coaching association, particularly if they claim to be one of the founders. When corporate leaders have made the career transition from executive to coach, they often cite having themselves experienced a transformational coaching moment as the main motivator in making that transition. Their passionate wish is to do for others what was so wonderfully done for them, at that moment of enlightenment.

In conclusion, while the valorisation of clients as heroes may seem like an innocent and well-intentioned practice, it raises significant concerns. The power dynamics, unrealistic expectations, inflated egos, ethical concerns, and damage to the coaching profession all highlight the potential negative impact of this trend. Coaches and coaching associations, in an ethical world, need to remain vigilant and prioritise the growth and well-being of their clients over their own desire for recognition or status. Ultimately, it could be argued that the success of coaching lies in its ability to empower leaders, not to overshadow them, nor to seek to leverage their relationship with their clients for commercial advantage.

The suggestive power of Foundation Stories.

One signifier of organisations' entry to the maturity phase is their preoccupation with crafting the narrative of their foundation stories, retrospectively. This focus has proved particularly true of those coaching associations where the founders – or those that claim to be the founders – remain in role, either as current executives or in titular or honorary roles. These signifiers include self-administrated lifelong memberships and ambassadorships, bequeathing upon the chosen ones the licence to travel to far flung territories to proclaim the word. The foundation stories related on such crusades served both to enhance the carefully constructed venerability of the associations, as well as to reify the brand of these missionary founding fathers (as they were most often men) as they transitioned from their early messiah incarnation to grandee status. Within these foundation stories, history is written by the victors. Those who had fallen by the wayside in power struggles or ideological skirmishes were surgically removed from the history, consigned to ghost ships occasionally glimpsed as they passed through committee rooms, but rarely referenced.

Foundation stories are a key element in the formation of organisation identity, serving as the basis for their existence by providing a narrative that justifies and motivates their actions. What then are the foundation stories that are promulgated by coaching associations? The first and most common foundation story centres around the belief that, for putative coaches, there is a clear knowledge gap that needs to be filled; and coaching associations claim that their expertise is essential in bridging this gap and guiding individuals towards success. While this may seem like a noble endeavour, it raises the question of why such a gap exists in the first place. Are educational systems failing us? Have other personal development efforts fallen short? The emphasis on this knowledge gap among foundation narratives suggests that there are systemic issues that need to be addressed, beyond individual skills development.

This' bridging the gap' foundation story revolves around the idea that everyone has untapped potential waiting to be unleashed. Coaching associations often claim that their methods and tools can unlock this potential, helping individuals achieve greatness. However, this narrative overlooks the fact that not everyone desires or needs to reach their maximum potential. Does everyone need to strive for greatness? Isn't it okay to be content and find fulfilment in a simple, ordinary life? The obsession with unlocking untapped potential may lead to a constant sense of dissatisfaction and an unending pursuit of unattainable goals, together with a low-grade sense of guilt or a resentment at feeling perpetually pushed towards greater heights. It may even be that in reality there is no discernible gap in the first place, as for example in the myth that we only use about 60% of the capacity of our brains, while neuroscience would suggest that most of our brain is at full capacity, most of the time. Yet the 'gap' narrative continues to freight a powerful marketing hook that few find easy to resist.

A reinforcing foundation story centres on the belief that individuals are solely responsible for their own success or failure. Coaching associations often portray themselves as the key to unlocking personal accountability and self-improvement. Whilst it is hard to argue against the idea that taking responsibility for one's actions is central to personal efficacy, this narrative overlooks the influence of external factors such as socio-economic background, systemic barriers, and plain old good luck. The insistence on individual responsibility may lead to an inferential blaming and shaming process, where those who fail are seen as lacking effort or character, further exacerbating existing inequalities.

A prevalent foundation story is that coaching associations possess a unique and exclusive set of skills and knowledge, creating a sense of superiority, suggesting that it is only through attachment to them that success will achieved. However, this claim raises concerns about the accessibility and affordability of coaching services. It perpetuates a hierarchical structure where success becomes the privilege of those who can afford such coaching. This exclusivity undermines the idea of equal opportunities for all and reinforces existing power dynamics.

In addition, coaching bodies often share the foundation story that there is a universal formula or blueprint for success. This narrative disregards the infinite complexities and unique circumstances of individuals' lives. It overlooks the fact that success can mean different things to different people. The reliance on a one-size-fits-all approach may lead individuals to feel inadequate or misunderstood if they are unable to fit into the predefined mould of success.

Every coaching association has crafted its own elaborate foundation story, weaving the generic foundation stories elaborated above into an account of how it all began for their particular association, accompanied by detailed, mythic narratives of the journey taken to get where it the story is today. These stories are often embellished with heroic accounts of the daring do of their pioneering fathers who started from humble beginnings and rose to their current exalted heights, creating an illusion a path to success that might be attainable to all. These foundation stories are often presented as linear narratives, conveniently omitting the countless setbacks, failures, and sacrifices that were made along the way. They seldom mention those leaders who fell on the way, were removed, or chose to step aside.

Through the selective representation of success stories, founding coaches often highlight their most exceptional client successes, of those who have achieved remarkable feats in a relatively short period. This cherry-picking of success stories may create unrealistic expectations and reinforce the idea that rapid success is the norm, leaving others feeling inadequate or discouraged when they do not achieve similar outcomes. By oversimplifying the process, aspiring individuals may be misled into believing that success is easily attainable without fully understanding the challenges they may face.

These stories often focus on individual triumph rather than acknowledging the societal factors that may have played a role in their success. While personal grit and determination are undoubtedly essential, the coaching industry tends to downplay the significance of structural advantages such as access to resources, networks, and opportunities. By neglecting to mention these systemic factors, individuals may feel disheartened or inadequate when faced with similar circumstances. Furthermore, the coaching industry's stories tend to exaggerate the transformative power of coaching itself. While coaching can undoubtedly be beneficial, it is important to acknowledge that it is not a one-size-fits-all solution. Personal growth and success are multifaceted, and individuals may require a combination of different resources, skills, and support systems to achieve their goals. By overselling the impact of coaching alone, people may become disillusioned and blame themselves when they don't experience the same drastic improvements as those highlighted in these narratives.

The pressure to conform to societal expectations of success can also contribute to the exaggeration of foundation stories. Contemporary society generally views success as having achieved great things within a short period of time. To meet these expectations, coaching bodies may feel compelled to embellish their origins and milestones, creating a false sense of rapid progress towards seemly impossible goals. However, in doing so, they perpetuate a culture of fakery and undermine the value of genuine, sustainable growth. The lack of accountability within the coaching industry plays a significant role in the embellishment of foundation stories. Without proper regulations and oversight, coaching bodies are free to fabricate narratives without facing consequences. This absence of accountability enables the continued propagation of misleading stories, harming not only potential clients but also the credibility of the entire coaching profession.

The coaching associations foundation stories often lack diversity and fail to represent a range of experiences. By primarily showcasing stories of individuals who have managed to achieve material wealth or fame, coaching bodies inadvertently promote a narrow definition of success. While typical foundation stories told by coaching associations may appear as heroic tales, on closer analysis these accounts reveal a conspicuous lack of nuance and accuracy. The oversimplification, omission of structural factors, exaggeration of coaching impact, selective representation of success, and lack of diversity all contribute to a distorted narrative that may mislead individuals and set unrealistic expectations as the choose to join such associations.

Added to this oversimplification sits an inclination to lionise their founders is the tendency for selective omission of historical context. The practice of retrofitting post-hoc foundation stories introduces a concerning bias, prioritising certain narratives and perspectives, further marginalizing alternative viewpoints and voices within the coaching community. By elevating their leaders to a pedestal, coaching bodies risk stifling dissent and discourage critical thinking. Foundation stories often paint a rosy picture of the current leader's involvement and impact. By conveniently leaving out the contributions of past leaders and the collective efforts of the coaching community, these stories effectively rewrite history. They often attribute game-changing innovations and sweeping changes solely to the current leader's genius and vision. While leaders undoubtedly leave their mark on organisations, it is misleading to suggest that everything achieved is solely their doing. This exaggeration creates an atmosphere of hero-worship, obscuring the contributions of the larger coaching community and reinforcing a cult of personality around the leader.

To what extent is the continual recitation of these foundation stories harmful to the integrity of the profession? Firstly, it proves harmful because coaching associations strongly feel the need to showcase their importance and relevance in the industry. By exaggerating their origins and achievements, they hope to gain credibility and establish themselves as authority figures in the field. However, this quest for recognition comes at the cost of honesty and transparency. The fear of competition contributes to the embellishment of foundation stories. In a highly competitive landscape, coaching associations are constantly vying for clients and recognition. By creating an exaggerated foundation narrative, they hope to differentiate themselves from their competitors and attract more attention.

By fabricating an impressive foundation story, coaching bodies aim to attract more clients and increase their profit margins. These grandiose tales often appeal to potential clients who may be more inclined to trust a coaching body with a seemingly remarkable history and a compelling story to tell.

What different types of credential consumer are there?

This chapter is based on a longitudinal survey of coaches conducted by the Critical Coaching Group between 2012 and 2019. This survey identified seven principal types of potential consumers at the ***pre-purchase stage***, briefly described below.

1. **Enthusiasts** are highly enamoured of the good that coaching can do in the world, and are keen to get on with the process of being credentialed, to enable them to be the best they could possibly be, as quickly as possible.
2. **Compliers** want to do the right thing. They often worry that because they have come into coaching from a non-business background, that they will be somehow 'found out' by clients, or by established professionals and their constituent bodies. A concern regarding 'impostor syndrome', and of being 'not good enough' is often prevalent among this grouping.

3. **Susceptibles** are influenced by the claims made by credential providers, with extravagant promises made for high earnings post accreditation. Susceptibles may have been tempted to go on a 'free' taster day, and have signed up while under pressure to close the sale. They may have been made redundant, or in receipt of a financial pay-off, and were looking to invest in a new career, without reality-checking the coaching market.
4. **Pragmatists** are relatively unconcerned about the competing merits of the various credentials on offer. They wish to take the most direct line between the starting point and qualification, while minimising the time and financial investment required.
5. **Procrastinators** tend to delay their purchase in the face of the multiple and conflicting array of credentials on offer. They will not make a move until they know that their money is safely invested – or else at the point where the market or the government demands that they comply.
6. **Agnostics** already have a well-established coaching business and have never felt the need to be credentialed. They are cynical of attempts to persuade coaches to invest in what they often describe in 'pyramid schemes' whose main covert goal is to make training providers and coaching gurus rich at the

expense of insecure entrants to the market existing at the bottom of the sales pyramid.

7. **Ideologues** push against the professionalising of coaching, which they contend runs in the face of the inclusive and emancipatory origins of coaching. They worry that much of the contemporary research into coaching is driven by market forces, and subject to confirmation bias. They are concerned that Business Schools, in their wish to climb aboard the coaching provision bandwagon, are prey to alliances with predatory providers and a variety of unregulated professional bodies.

8. **Inquirers** are curiosity driven, restless to understand their inner and outer worlds as coaches. They rate reflective practice as indispensable in the route towards gaining credentials. While they often valorise credentials over accreditations, they can choose, especially early on, the choose pursuing accreditation for instrumental reasons, while valorising the inquiry process.

Shifts in the credentialing landscape over the six years embraced by the survey encouraged a running of the same survey, with broadly the same population, in 2020, where many of the respondents were now well into the **post-purchase stage.** This is what was found.

Enthusiasts began their credentialing journey with high hopes, believing that they had made a good purchasing decision. Evidence suggests that while many enthusiasts had their original optimism reinforced, others confessed to background doubts regarding the efficacy of their decision, but were still pleased to have the badge. Some have gone to collect further badges, while others have been dismayed to see the never-ending mountain range of credential horisons stretching ahead, beyond credentials base-camp.

The **compliers** followed the credentialing process sedulously. Having secured accreditation, some compliers argue for further tightening of regulation and standards. Many have graduated to serve in formal professional roles where they assess the 'licence to operate' of fellow coaches. They express strong support for the need for compulsory supervision, while many have gone on to qualify and practice as supervisors and craft supervisor training offerings.

The **pragmatists**, content to have secured the badge, now do the minimum to maintain that badge. Some are not that happy with the renewal merry-go-round - with its increasing ramping-up of requirement for CPD and supervision - to the extent that, having established their business, are considering relinquishing their badge.

The **susceptibles**, more than other groups, became disillusioned at an early stage by the commoditised nature of their provider's learning provision. As few of the promises of business growth ever eventuated, then susceptibles became subject to deep levels of buyer remorse. Business School offerings were not immune to such degrees of disillusionment among susceptibles.

The **procrastinators** continue to equivocate, beyond the concession of gaining token membership of a professional body. When they see others making purchasing mistakes, they feel smug, turning their prevarication into a virtue. Some feel mild existential anxiety around their lack of credentials, but not enough to propel action.

The **agnostics** are further cemented in their suspicions that the drive to professionalisation, far from being in service of enhancing coaching quality, is clandestinely designed to create pyramided cartels. Their clients continue to take them as they find them, and to recommend them on, which is the primary source of their business getting.

The **ideologues** witness further evidence of the increasing damage that professionalisation and marketisation do to the original emancipatory thrust of coaching, as the drive towards 'neo-feudalism' gains speed. They have a feeling that they are becoming an endangered species on the coaching landscape, even among Business School colleagues.

The **inquirers** may have discovered a practice that fits for them, such as 'clean coaching' or 'transpersonal' and decide to deepen that signature niche: or, more likely, their innate restlessness has directed them towards alternative ways of seeing and enacting coaching. Their pursuit is of emergent learning , and they seek out fellow travelers to make sense of what can be a lonely road; though they may create alternative badges of recognition, but not for the purpose of CPD accretion.

Across all these categories, respondents reported that while professional bodies and training providers strongly imply that clients may ask for evidence of membership of a professional body, and of a minimum level of training, there is very little evidence from these respondents' experiences to suggest that clients **require** such; nor is there evidence that clients purchasing decisions are overly swayed by prospective coaches displaying a long string of credentials.

These findings would suggest that for **enthusiasts, for compliers** and for **susceptibles**, that they shop around before they take the credentialing plunge, concentrating on business growth by organic means before investing in glossy programmes or accreditations that promise visibility in the market. They would be advised to seeking out a mentor who knows the field well, and to network with peers who are on the path. To this end, joining a professional body is one way into building alliances and seeking support, without needing to start credentialling until they are sure that the path you choose is one best suited to ones needs. Above all, it is important to claim agency for personal developmental decisions, rather than to feel pressured by illusory regulations and persuasive salespeople's inflated claims into premature purchase.

For **prevaricators**, choosing not to participate remains an option and will continue into the foreseeable future. Agnostics and Idealogues need no further encouragement to remain on the margins, but they might be attracted to act in a mentoring role to new entrants who are feeling their way into a compressed market and need voices of caution and critical perspective as much as those of unmitigated encouragement.

For the **inquirers,** the advice, should advice be needed of heeded, would be to keep seeking out fresh perspectives and alternative thinking partners, and not to be afraid to transgress. A warning would be to be alert to the temptation to codify and create standard trainings, including setting levels of seniority for your freshly minted alternative practice.

For those of an **entrepreneurial** inclination, then it is unlikely that coaching individual clients will feed that commercial appetite. Entrepreneurs concentrate on building a distinct brand; creating products that are novel and on trend; writing a book that serves as a sophisticated business card; building alliances with professional bodies and celebrity coaches all serve to grow business, which is likely to have at its heart coach training and supervision as opposed to direct coaching of clients alone.

The credentials 'arms race:' premature selling of novel products.

In the hypercompetitive market for members, the professional bodies began to engage in a credentials 'arms race.' This escalation of award offerings has meant a corresponding growth in credential training among competing training providers for each of these emergent categories. While the professional bodies may claim that this growth is demand driven, there is strong evidence of supply push. Beyond the boundaries of these self-styled professional associations, there appeared a profusion of additional providers making claims for their alternative trainings; claims for marketability that go far beyond the intrinsic learning so gained. The string of credentials for sale that many providers display is designed to both impress and incite an appetite for the same among coaches. It is instructive to scan the profiles of officers and ambassadors of professional associations and providers for evidence of the myriad array of credential signifiers strung behind their names, such as 'EMCC IPMA Master Practitioner, EMCC EIA Senior Practitioner.'

Across these coaching associations, the pursuit of perpetual novelty and innovation seems to have reached an alarming level. These organisations often introduce new products, methodologies, and approaches without adequate validation, in a hasty rush to market. While this fast tracking may seem like an exciting and promising endeavour to some, it is essential to question the efficacy and long-term impact of this bombardment of newness on ordinary members.

New ideas and practices can bring about positive change and enhance the effectiveness of coaching bodies. However, it is equally crucial to strike a balance between innovation and validation. Without proper validation, these new products and methodologies may end up being nothing more than empty promises or trendy fads, failing to deliver real value to their users. One of the primary effects of this rush to embrace perpetual novelty is the confusion it creates among ordinary members. With this constant deluge of new offerings, members may feel overwhelmed, unsure of which products or approaches are truly beneficial and which are just fleeting trends. This confusion can lead to a loss of trust in coaching association as members struggle to discern what is genuine and what is merely a gimmick – while feeling that their current hard-won credential is now rendered obsolete.

Moreover, by continuously chasing after the 'next big thing,' coaching associations risk neglecting the laying down of solid foundations and underlying principles. While it is essential to remain open to new ideas and trends, adopting them without proper validation can sideline tried-and-tested methods that have withstood the test of time. Ultimately, this can undermine the credibility and reliability of coaching associations, as members may start questioning the organisation's commitment to providing value over hype. Furthermore, the rush to market without validation can lead to unethical practices. When a coaching association actively copies other organisations or rushes to release products, it prioritises competition over integrity. By sacrificing proper validation, these organisations may be compromising the quality and safety of their offerings. This not only puts members at risk but also damages the reputation and ethical standing of the coaching profession.

Without proper validation or testing, there is no guarantee that the product or service being offered provides the intended benefits or produces the desired results. This could lead to ordinary members wasting their time, energy, and money on ineffective coaching. It could also mean them being exposed to harmful or unsafe practices, putting their well-being at risk. It can also mean wasted resources. Rushing to market without validation or testing can mean that coaching association invest resources in developing and marketing a product that ultimately fails or proves to be unsuccessful. This wasted investment can result in financial losses for the organisation, potentially affecting their ability to provide quality coaching services in the future.

Despite these limitations, coaching association may make misleading or false claims about the effectiveness or benefits of their products. This can lead to ordinary members making decisions based on inaccurate information, resulting in disappointment or harm. Ordinary members may lose faith in the coaching association, and this loss of trust can be difficult to regain. If their products or services cause harm or if they have made false claims, they could face legal action and further damage their reputation in the industry.

In summary, the rush to bring new coaching products to market without proper validation or testing can lead to ineffective coaching, wasted resources, harm to ordinary members, misleading claims, damage to trust and reputation, as well as legal and ethical implications. While innovation is essential for the growth of coaching, rushing to introduce new products without validation poses significant risks. This bombardment of novelty can only lead to confusion, a loss of trust, neglect of proven methods, and a decline in ethical practices.

Quantity trumping quality in coaching associations' priorities.

What matters can't be measured: what can be measured doesn't matter.

The world of professional coaching associations has undergone a significant shift in recent years, morphing into a race for quantity and profit. The focus on quantity over quality is evident in the emerging proliferation of coaching certifications and accreditation bodies. In today's market, it seems like anyone with a few hours to spare can become a certified coach. Numerous associations offer quick and inexpensive courses that promise a shiny certificate upon completion. This influx of coaches flooding the market dilutes the pool of genuinely qualified professionals, making it difficult for clients to distinguish between those with valuable expertise and those with mere paper credentials.

Secondly, the emphasis on quantity is noticeable in the way coaching associations prioritise mass enrolment and rapid certification over selective recruitment and diligent certification. It is not uncommon to see associations boasting about the number of coaches they have trained rather than their success rates or the impact that this education has had on their clients. The desire to churn out as many certified coaches as possible undermines the time and effort required for true mastery of the coaching craft. Instead of nurturing a select few highly skilled practitioners, the focus has shifted to producing a large quantity of (perhaps) minimally trained individuals.

This shift towards quantity over quality is perpetuated by the industry's reliance on marketing tactics and member acquisition. Motivated by economic growth imperatives, coaching associations employ aggressive marketing strategies to attract as many potential clients and students as possible. This emphasis on revenue generation often comes at the expense of comprehensive education and the development of professional standards. The coaching industry has become more about selling an illusion of success rather than genuinely supporting personal growth and development.

Moreover, the rise of online coaching platforms and digital courses has further fuelled the quantity-focused mindset. With the convenience and accessibility offered by technology, coaching can now be delivered at scale. While there are undoubtedly benefits to this democratisation of coaching, it also allows for the mass production of coaches. Virtual coaching sessions lack the depth and interpersonal connection that can be achieved through face-to-face interactions, compromising the quality of the coaching experience. The rush to embrace technology has inadvertently resulted in a decline in quality coaching and personalised support.

Lastly, the pressure to keep up with the demand for quantity has led to a dangerous erosion of ethical practices within the coaching industry. Coaching associations, ever eager to secure members and generate income, may exaggerate unrealistic outcomes. This can lead to disappointment and disillusionment for members who were led to believe in false promises. Furthermore, the lack of stringent oversight and regulation in the coaching world enables unqualified individuals to operate freely, potentially causing harm to vulnerable clients seeking guidance and support.

Associated with the drive for quantity over quality is a growing fixation with novelty, further promoting the trend for superficiality over depth. When aspiring coaches are encouraged to accumulate many credentials quickly, they may overlook the importance of investing time and effort into in-depth learning and mastery. On top of that, a constant quest for novelty can breed a culture that values change for the sake of change, often disregarding its efficacy. While new coaching practices can offer fresh perspectives, not every novel approach will yield positive outcomes. Some may prove ineffective or even detrimental to client progress. By blindly embracing novelty, coaching associations risk sacrificing the safety and effectiveness achieved through rigorous evaluation of established methodologies.

Placing an excessive emphasis on novelty and innovation can distract from the ethical aspects of coaching. Ethical guidelines, which are typically grounded in tried and trusted practices, ensure that coaches prioritise the well-being and confidentiality of their clients. By touting novelty as a primary concern, coaching associations may inadvertently allow the neglect of these ethical principles, potentially exposing clients to harm or violating their trust. Prioritising novelty over the tried and trusted can discourage coaches from engaging in meaningful continuous professional development. By constantly seeking the next breaking trend, many coaches may fail to invest adequate time and effort in refining their existing skills and building a strong foundation. This neglect of lifelong learning inhibits the growth and maturation of coaching as a profession, hindering its potential to positively impact clients' lives.

Members of professional coaching associations may have mixed feelings about the shift towards a focus on novelty and innovation, and on quantity, but for many it is difficult to resist the attractions of the latest fad and fashion. While this valorising of innovation may suit those coaches eager to quickly attain badges or signifiers to promote themselves as conversant with the latest trends, it can leave others feeling disregarded and even stigmatised, especially those who seek a more narrative and reflective coaching experience.

The appetite for novelty is not solely driven by supply push from first adopters among associations and training providers. It is important to acknowledge the demand pull for innovative approaches exercised by certain clients both at the individual and corporate level. And then there are the clients who are driven by the desire for quick and tangible results, when the conventional tried and trusted approaches may appear too time-consuming or outdated to them. For such clients, the focus on speed also allows them to access a wide range of coaching experiences, enabling them to explore a variety of techniques in a shorter time span through a coalition of innovation and speedy delivery.

However, while this shift towards the promotion of fast-track innovation among coaching associations may be beneficial for some coaches, it inadvertently alienates another group of coaches who are often drawn to coaching as a means of personal growth and self-discovery, and prefer to deliver to their clients a coaching experience that is more narrative and reflective in nature. By focusing on novelty and innovation, professional coaching associations risk neglecting the need for more meaningful and introspective experiences. Baseline coaching practices such as listening, summarising, challenging, supporting, become subject to being rendered as complicated, grid-based practices that are amenable to quantifiable measurement, rather than the slow burn approach that suits them best.

Reflective Practice endangered by speed-learning imperatives.

This incessant pursuit of novelty and innovation can inadvertently create an environment where the importance of reflective coaching is questioned or even gently stigmatised as being too soft and woo woo. This can lead to doubts and self-questioning for such coaches, who may begin to internalise the belief that their preference for a slower, more introspective coaching style is somehow inadequate or less valuable. As a result, they may find themselves questioning their own needs and desires, and may even start to doubt the validity of their experiences and perspectives.

While this fad-based approach may suit certain clients and association members who prioritise quick signifiers and self-promotion, it simultaneously highlights the contradictory nature of claiming to promote the acquisition of reflective practice alongside processes built for speed and superficiality, without too much due diligence occurring before the product goes to market. Reflective practice, a fundamental principle advocated by coaching bodies, encourages individuals to engage in deep introspection and examination of their thoughts, emotions, and behaviours. However, a focus on novelty and innovation often prioritises surface-level techniques that lack the depth required for meaningful transformation.

Sustainable personal development arises from a deep understanding of oneself and the ability to critically evaluate and challenge existing beliefs and behaviours. One of the primary concerns that arise when coaching associations fail to prioritise deep reflective practice is the erosion of authenticity and trustworthiness. Without engaging in self-reflection, coaches may unintentionally carry their personal biases, unresolved issues, or blind spots into their coaching sessions. This lack of self-awareness and authenticity undermines the trust clients should have in their coaches, potentially damaging the coach-client relationship and diminishing the effectiveness of coaching as a whole.

Deep reflective practice allows coaches to critically examine their coaching methods, techniques, and approaches. When coaching associations neglect this inner inquiry, coaches may resort to superficial problem-solving techniques. Instead of encouraging clients' personal growth and self-discovery, coaches might focus solely on short-term fixes or quick solutions, and rely on the received wisdom of their associations. This approach limits the transformative potential of coaching, depriving clients of sustainable change and personal development. Deep reflective practice helps coaches recognise their own strengths, weaknesses, and blind spots. This self-awareness forms the foundation for authentic coaching relationships built on trust and empathy. When coaches prioritise introspection, they can better support clients' growth journeys and create a safe space for exploration and vulnerability. The truism that declares 'that the capacity to develop others is limited by the extent to which one is prepared to push one's own developmental edges' is highly salient in this respect.

An essential component of coaching is providing clients with valuable assessments and constructive feedback. However, when coaching associations neglect deep reflective practice, there is a risk of ineffective and biased evaluation. Coaches need to reflect on their own biases, assumptions, and potential blind spots that could influence their feedback. Failure to prioritise deep reflective practice may result in superficial evaluations, hindering clients' progress and limiting the impact of coaching interventions, while seeming to serve up plausible metrics.

A cornerstone of the coaching profession is the idea that coaches possess expertise, enabling them to guide and support clients effectively, a cornerstone that is challengeable as marketing hype. However, without deep reflective practice, this expertise becomes exposed as nothing more than an illusion it is, True expertise in coaching lies not in a mere accumulation of knowledge but in the ability to reflect on one's biases, assumptions, and experiences. By neglecting deep reflection, coaching associations risk fostering a false sense of mastery among their practitioners, leading to a lack of genuine understanding and empathy for clients. Instead, the clients may merely have their own underlying assumptions and defensive routines reinforced.

Engaging in deep reflection helps coaches explore their ethical stance, biases, and how these factors may influence their coaching relationships. Ethical dilemmas arise when coaches fail to recognise and address their own limitations and ingrained biases. Neglecting deep reflective practice may lead to coaches inadvertently promoting harmful beliefs or approaches, eroding the trust clients place in their coaching relationships – or worse inculcating a false trust that is based in a fragile surface of certainty and reassurance. The coaching field often promotes the idea of success, confidence, and certainty – which has its own virtues – it may obviate clients navigating their own insecurities and vulnerabilities.

Without encouraging critical self-reflection, coaching associations may inadvertently foster a culture of stagnation.

This can stifle growth, limit opportunities for professional development, and prevent coaching from adapting to the changing needs and demands of clients. Ultimately, neglecting deep reflective practice denies the coaching industry the potential for continued progress and advancement. Deep reflective practice plays a pivotal role in identifying ethical dilemmas, biases, and conflicts of interest that can arise during coaching engagements. By not prioritising this practice, coaching associations might inadvertently foster unethical behaviour, potentially causing harm to clients. The absence of critical self-reflection may lead to an ethical vacuum within the coaching industry, undermining its credibility and perpetuating harm instead of facilitating growth.

While coaching associations, by and large, pay lip-service to reflective practice among its members, it may well be that in some ways they shy away from deeper adherence to it. Could this be because deep introspection by lay members may well give rise to challenges to their own shibboleths of innovation and empirically based certainty? A little learning is a dangerous thing. The promotion of deep reflection may cause some clients to deeply question the worthwhileness of their jobs. It may also cause some coaches to question their role in reinforcing managerial precepts among their clients – and not only among their clients but also in the neo-feudal management of their coaching associations also.

The impact of digitalisation on centralisation of control

In a world where commercial growth is imperative for survival, reliance on algorithm-based services and centralisation of control has become the norm. However, in this pursuit for efficiency and profit, the human factor, in common with many other organisations, is being stripped away from coaching associations. Coaching, once a profession rooted in personal connections and empathy, is gradually losing its essence. Algorithms, designed to maximise efficiency and productivity, have started to play a pivotal role in the coaching industry. These algorithms analyse vast amounts of data, evaluating performance and providing recommendations based on predetermined criteria. As a result, coaching is in danger of becoming highly formulaic, devoid of the intangible aspects which make it a meaningful endeavour.

One of the primary concerns with algorithm-based coaching is the lack of individualised attention. These systems treat every association member as a data point, failing to consider the uniqueness of human experiences and emotions. A one-size-fits-all approach disregards the intricate web of personal circumstances that shape an individual's needs and aspirations. The human factor, with its capacity for sensitivity and understanding, is far better equipped to comprehend and address the complexities of human existence than any algorithm no matter how sophisticated.

Moreover, the centralisation of control in coaching associations exacerbates the digitalisation problem. As coaching becomes more standardised, power is concentrated in the hands of a few individuals who dictate the practices and procedures, in a neo-feudalistic fashion. This centralisation restricts the autonomy of coaches, reducing them to mere executors of predefined methods and approaches. The creativity and flexibility that was once a hallmark of coaching are stifled under the weight of rigid guidelines, leaving little room for personal growth and innovation.

The consequences of this trend are far-reaching, affecting not only those seeking guidance but also the coaches themselves. Individual clients who turn to coaching are often in vulnerable states, seeking assistance in navigating life's challenges. However, algorithm-based services often fail to provide the emotional support necessary for personal growth. Psychometric tests are no substitute for a living person listening to what is on your mind. The absence of genuine human interaction and understanding can leave individuals feeling isolated and misunderstood, exacerbating their struggles instead of alleviating them.

On the other hand, coaching associations are also victims of the commercial growth imperative. Coaches, once considered trusted experts in their field, are reduced to mere cogs in a profit-driven machine. Their expertise and intuition are undervalued and undermined, reducing their profession to a series of tick-boxes and metrics. The erosion of the human factor erodes the credibility and efficacy of the coaching profession as a whole.

Infantilisation and creation of a fear culture

There are several forces that might driving coaching professional association towards infantilising their members, within the loose definition that infantilisation is to treat someone as if that person were a child, with the result that they start behaving like one. The same can apply at the collective level as well as at the level of the individual. A few possible factors driving infantilisation might include regulation and standardization, where the setting of stringent standards and regulations to ensure consistency and quality in the field. This can result in an overemphasis on rules and requirements, which may make members feel like they are being treated as children, allied to concerns regarding risk management and legal liabilities. By imposing strict guidelines and control measures, they may aim to protect both the coaches and the clients, these measures can inadvertently make members feel controlled and limited in their professional autonomy.

Coaching professional associations, in line with any professional organisation, strive to maintain the credibility and reputation of their field. They may view standardization and tight controls as essential to positioning coaching as a credible and serious profession. This can lead to a focus on enforcing compliance, which can sometimes feel patronising and infantilising to members. Coaching is a relatively new profession that continues to evolve. Professional association may feel the need to establish a sense of professionalism and propriety, which can involve imposing strict codes of conduct and ethical guidelines to compensate for this lack of form. However, if these guidelines are excessively restrictive and rigid, it may give members the impression that they are being treated as children incapable of self-regulation.

Excessive application of strategies that foster infantilisation may result in feelings of incompetence and dependency among members, who could be led to doubt their abilities and feel incapable of making decisions or taking independent action. This could erode their self-confidence and create a sense of dependency on the professional association for guidance. On the other hand, being treated in an infantilising manner may result in members feeling frustrated or dissatisfied with their professional association and cause them to act in a counter-dependent manner, perceiving such treatment as disrespectful, disempowering, or patronising.

Infantilisation can potentially drive members to disengage from the professional association's activities and initiatives. If they feel their contributions are undervalued or that their autonomy is consistently undermined, they may lose interest in participating actively, leading to a decline in overall engagement. If members perceive their professional association as operating through fear tactics, such as punishment or intimidation, the creation of a fear culture may create an environment where individuals are afraid to question decisions, take risks, or voice concerns.

Coaching associations, by their nature, should serve as a support system for their members, fostering growth and professional development. However, when an atmosphere of infantilisation emerges, individuals may find themselves disempowered and stripped of their autonomy. As a result, fear becomes deeply embedded within the organisation, stifling creativity, innovation, and meaningful dialogue. Paradoxically, while these association espouse values of openness and inclusion, they often struggle to manage the dissonance created by their approach to managing their members. If the leaders of such associations react to push backs against infantilisation by increasing control measures that inspire fear among their members and volunteers, then this can escalate to the point where a full-blown fear culture is instilled, when members fear making challenges as they may be subject to reprisals.

The dissonance between the espoused values of openness and inclusion and the reality of the infantilising culture within coaching association raises the question as to how these association manage this inconsistency. One way they attempt to address this dissonance is by implementing token gestures of inclusivity, such as diversity and inclusion training sessions, or the creation of committees specifically aimed at promoting diversity. While these initiatives have good intentions, they often fail to address the root issue of infantilisation. To truly bridge this gap, coaching association should strive to shift their focus towards empowering and supporting their members as equals, rather than perpetuating a hierarchical power structure, but this would seem to require a paradigm shift of which there is little evidence within several coaching associations, despite the façade of inclusiveness.

Ironically, most coaching associations strive to promote openness and inclusion as core values. They emphasise the importance of diversity, respect, and collaboration, aiming to create an environment that nurtures personal and professional growth. However, the disconnect arises when these values are not consistently reflected in the behaviours and practices of the association themselves. The dissonance occurs due to a misalignment between the desired principles and the structures or procedures that preserve control and hierarchy.

Entering the maturation stage of association development.

The reality behind dependence on a volunteer base.

While the 'volunteer defence' was allowed for by forgiving members in the early pioneering days of such associations, members' tolerance grew less elastic as the sophistication of the associations' offerings expanded, and the failures to subsequently deliver upon rising expectations became more acute. For those whose selfless followership instinct ran deep, these long-suffering volunteers allowed the increasing demands on their goodwill to persist for quite some time. For other more self-protective volunteers there was evidence of an increasing groundswell of low-grade resentment among them that they were being put upon, and that their psychological contract with the association was at breaking point, with little coming back to them by way of compensation for their efforts.

For others, resting on top of that sense that they were being exploited, was a growing uneasiness that they were supporting something that was ultimately inimical to their personal ethical code, given the way they perceived their leadership to be conducting themselves, not least in the commercial arena, where they could be perceived as pursuing growth at all costs. With that realisation, such volunteers moved away, in whole or in part, both through overload, burnout, and through disillusionment born of the cognitive dissonance between their aspirations as what they were being asked to do, and what they believed they had been brought in to do in the first place, in good faith. While this loss of volunteers undoubtedly caused momentary discomfort and operational disruption to the leaders of the associations, they drew succour from that fact that there was always a wave of fresh volunteers willing and able to fill these vacancies, who were susceptible to flattery and 'love bombing.'

In fact, many of the chosen declared, via web profiles, that they were honoured to answer the call to serve, and to have the opportunity to 'give back.' Therefore, it was through such apparently seamless replacement that the associations were able to grow without too much internal dissent or questioning of the underlying assumptions driving the growth of the association. The continual overlay of 'positivity' as a foundation stone of coaching practice meant that retreating officers expressing doubts as to the association's true prospectus could be easily dismissed as being 'negative.'

It can be argued that there began to develop - certainly in a number of these associations - a fear-driven culture where members and volunteer workers became infantilised by their leaders, who demanded dependence from them. The creation of virtual control mechanisms and processes – such as imposing performance management measures on its volunteer officers using KPIs (Key Performance Indicators) - reinforce this creation of an infantilised upward facing culture.

Countering the Volunteerism Defence: unmasking high control tactics

Volunteerism is a noble concept that exemplifies selflessness and community spirit. It is a cornerstone of many not-for-profit organisations, including coaching associations. However, when leaders of coaching associations exploit this concept to justify their strategies then it becomes essential to critically examine the inherent flaws in their argument. Across all the coaching associations, their leaders proclaim that volunteers are the life blood of the organisation – that volunteerism is the spirit it that it runs on, the heart blood.

There seems little doubt that in the early pioneering days of these associations, that the functioning of these associations stayed true to this maxim. However, as they grew and become more managerial, then evidence of the exploitation of volunteer goodwill began to be exploited, as leaders of coaching associations became apologists for the view that higher control measures were necessary to ensure efficient management. This rational grew in some instances to inherent abuse of volunteers' generosity, by demanding excessive commitments, pushing unrealistic deadlines, and encroaching upon personal time. As volunteers' goodwill was exploited for the organisation's benefit, then it began to undermine the fundamental spirit of volunteerism, reducing it to mere labour for the sake of achieving leadership objectives.

Coaching association leaders often defended their high control measures by claiming that they are necessary for creating a cohesive team and maintaining organisational standards. However, this defence only serves to mask the creation of a culture of dependence. By monopolising decision-making power and maintaining tight control, leaders ensure that volunteers remain solely reliant on their guidance and approval.

Coaching association leaders often assert that high control measures are essential for maintaining consistency and uniformity. However, such measures inadvertently suppress diverse perspectives and dissenting opinions. By promoting a one-size-fits-all approach, leaders discourage volunteers from questioning existing practices, stifling creativity and hindering the organisation's ability to evolve. There is evidence of an acknowledgement that constructive criticism and alternative perspectives are the lifeblood of growth and progress within any organisation, including coaching bodies. They espouse the power of 'courageous conversations.' Yet within several coaching associations, there is evidence of suppression of dissent in the name of compliance.

In justifying their high control approach, leaders of coaching associations contend that sometimes volunteers need to willingly sacrifice their autonomy for the greater good. However, this argument overlooks the fact that autonomy is a vital component of personal development and empowerment. Volunteering should be an opportunity for individuals to learn, grow, and exercise agency, rather than resigning themselves to becoming mere passive followers. By eroding volunteers' autonomy, leaders deprive them of the chance to develop essential leadership skills and stifle their potential for personal growth. Leaders can also resort to coercive control to keep volunteers in line, including implicit or explicit threats of exclusion born of the creation of a fear culture.

Perhaps the most significant objection to the 'volunteerism defence' is that high control measures employed by coaching association leaders undermine the genuine spirit of volunteerism. The notion of volunteering rests on the values of choice, altruism, and community engagement. While these precepts continue to be rolled out, as a hook, at the enticement and recruitment of volunteer's stage, in the form of benign 'love bombing,' volunteers may soon learn that by imposing excessive control, leaders distort these values, turning volunteers into mere instruments to fulfil their own objectives.

This distorted version of volunteerism erodes the very essence of the concept, ultimately leaving volunteers disillusioned and dispirited. Any cognitive dissonance on behalf of the volunteers may be softened if they themselves accede to managerial imperatives; and also by the fact that the secondary hook is the inducement that the through the occupation of volunteer roles, their profiles will be enhanced, and their networks grown, their CPD gained at reduced rates. Perhaps more than any of this, there is the buzz od feeling that they are 'inside the narrative,' that they can speak to others with an authentic insider voice.

The Volunteer justification: Fostering Relational Exchanges over Transactional

Volunteerism is often seen as one of the noblest forms of service, carrying with it an inherent value of community support and welfare. Advocates for volunteering often argue that it fosters relational exchanges with members, thereby focusing on genuine connections rather than transactional interactions. One of the fundamental aspects of the volunteer justification lies in the premise that individuals engage in volunteer work predominantly out of compassion and a sincere desire to make a difference. Indeed, the realm of volunteering is rich with such altruistic motivations that foster relational exchanges. Volunteers often cultivate meaningful connections with the communities they serve, creating long-lasting bonds that transcend transactional exchanges, feeding and nurturing the individual.

A crucial aspect of relational exchanges in volunteering is the reciprocation and emotional attachment that develops between volunteers and the recipients of their service. Unlike transactional interactions, volunteers form deep emotional connections with colleagues and clients by investing their time, energy, and empathy in the welfare of others. This emotional investment often leads to the creation of lasting relationships, built on trust, understanding, and shared experiences. Volunteers often emphasise their lack of payment as a signifier of their selfless commitment to the cause. They say that they are 'giving back,' for free, and that such giving brings with it deep satisfactions.

Engaging in volunteer activities not only benefits others but also provides immense personal growth opportunities for the volunteers themselves. By interacting with different individuals from diverse backgrounds, volunteers are exposed to unique perspectives, challenges, and resilience. This exposure encourages personal growth, empathy, facilitating authentic relational exchanges that extend beyond mere transactions.

By contrast, transactional exchanges tend to be short-lived and oriented around immediate goals. In contrast, volunteers often commit to long-term relationships and engage in continuous support for community development. This longevity allows for sustained relational exchanges, enabling volunteers to witness the progress and growth of the organisation they serve. Such sustained involvement further solidifies the relational nature of volunteerism, as it extends beyond superficial interactions.

Volunteering is deeply linked to community building and social impact. When volunteers forge relational exchanges and invest themselves in community development, they foster a sense of belonging and unity. Relational volunteerism catalyses dialogue, trust, and collaboration, allowing communities to work together towards shared goals. Consequently, volunteers become an integral part of the community fabric, nurturing lasting connections and engendering reciprocal support.

At What point does the loyalty of volunteers snap?

While volunteers give their time, energy, and expertise selflessly, driven by the desire to make a positive impact on the lives of others there comes a breaking point, a threshold can occur where their loyalty can snap is due to a confluence of various factors. One point at which the loyalty of volunteers may snap is when there is a lack of appreciation and recognition for their efforts from the leadership. Volunteers dedicate their time and effort to coaching associations without expecting monetary compensation. Instead, they seek gratitude and a sense of accomplishment for their contributions, on top of intrinsic job satisfaction. When their efforts go unnoticed or unacknowledged by their leadership, volunteers may feel undervalued and unimportant. This neglect can foster resentment and lead to a diminished commitment to the organisation.

Secondly, when volunteers feel their voices are disregarded or that their opinions have little weight, their loyalty can quickly erode. Volunteers often possess unique insights and perspectives gained from their diverse backgrounds and experiences, making their input invaluable for any organisation. When they perceive a lack of respect for their ideas or a sense of tokenism, it can lead to frustration and disillusionment. Such tokenism can be experienced as patronising and can prove deeply corrosive.

Thirdly, another pivotal moment can occur when volunteers experience a lack of professional development or growth opportunities within coaching bodies, which they were sold as part of their psychological contract when they signed up. If they find their experiences stagnant or without room for growth, their loyalty may snap, without investment in their development, offering training, mentoring, and opportunities for skill enhancement.

Volunteers want to be informed and engaged, knowing their efforts align with the organisation's mission and goals. When this vital communication link is severed, mistrust and uncertainty may take its place. A significant tipping point occurs when volunteers experience burnout or excessive demands on their time and energy. Volunteers often juggle multiple responsibilities, and when the demands of coaching associations become overwhelming, they may face a breaking point.

High levels of stress and fatigue can lead to volunteers questioning their commitment and ultimately disengaging from the organisation. This sense of burn-out can be intensified when the volunteer joined to follow a particular interest or passion, only to find that their efforts have been redirected towards fulfilment of a priority that they are not particularly invested in, or even worse that they ethically question or are opposed to. They may even find their passion discounted or even derided by the leadership as naïve idealism, which can cause an erosive cynicism to set in regarding the intention and motivations of the leadership of the association.

hubris causing leaders failing to detect the volunteer tipping point

Hubris, or excessive self-confidence, in coaching association leaders can prevent them from recognising the looming tipping point where volunteer loyalty is lost. Leaders with unchecked hubris may dismiss volunteers' concerns or feedback provided by volunteers, believing their own ideas or methods to be superior. This dismissal prevents leaders from identifying the tipping point and rectifying the underlying issues. Hubristic leaders may be unwilling to acknowledge their own shortcomings, making it difficult for them to detect signals of declining volunteer loyalty and address prevalent issues promptly, driving leaders to resist adopting new strategies, incorporating feedback, or adapting to changing circumstances. This resistance further alienates volunteers and exacerbates the tipping point. If no succession plan is in place, then a sense of hubris and invulnerability intensifies within the leaders, who often fail to see challenges to their leadership until it is too late.

However, in volunteer-based associations, leaders know that its workers are not tithed by income, and that if they become so disheartened then they might choose to leave. In the leader's eyes there may even be an upside in the purging of long serving volunteers, ridding the association of a source of dissent while passing a message to those still in place 'pour encourage les autres.' And if their recruitment of new members is at a healthy level, then the leadership know the disillusioned can easily be replaced by fresh blood.

However, the loss of volunteers, while hoping to rely on a fresh tranche of enthusiastic newbies is not without its downsides. Initially, new volunteers may join due to a passionate interest in the mission of the association, or of a desire to introduce something new to the association portfolio. However, sustaining volunteers' involvement and commitment requires associations to cultivate a genuine connection between volunteers and the cause. Without this emotional bond, volunteers may lose interest over time, resulting in a potential loss that cannot be solely compensated for by new recruits. The causes that once strongly attracted longer serving volunteers may now be less appealing or relevant to a new generation, who notice quickly that their passions are not represented in a fashion that they could comfortably work under. The bond needs to be relational – and continue to be so rather than derogating to a transactional 'give-get' basis.

Deepening the journey into the later maturation stage for associations

The above generalised account marks the trajectory of coaching associations through the 'growth' stage of organisation development, broadly placed within the timeframe of 1992 – 2008, begging the question as to what occurred to these associations as they traversed this maturity phase, from 2008 towards the present day. While fully accepting the folly of generalising across such a range of diverse associations, certain common developmental patterns do emerge. This account does not claim to provide a comprehensive snapshot of all that has occurred in this late maturity phase; much of that is covered in detail in the book on which this essay is based. Rather, the intention here is to focus on emergent themes that speak to the now and point to the future.

One signifier of organisations' entry to the maturity phase is their preoccupation with crafting the narrative of their foundation stories. This proved particularly true of those coaching associations where the founders – or those that claim to be the founders – remain in role, either as current executives or in titular or honorary roles. These signifiers include self-administrated lifelong memberships and ambassadorships, bequeathing upon the chosen ones the licence to travel to far flung territories to proclaim the word. The foundation stories related on such travels served both to enhance the carefully constructed venerability of the associations, as well as to reify the brand of these missionary founding fathers (as they were most often men) as they transitioned from their early messiah incarnation to grandee status. Within these foundation stories, history is written by the victors. Those who had fallen by the wayside in power struggles or ideological skirmishes were surgically removed from the history, consigned to ghost ships occasionally glimpsed as they passed through committee rooms, but rarely referenced.

One common characteristic of the transition from organisational growth to the maturity phase lies in facing the 'founder's dilemma,' where entry to the growth phase – in which revenue and costs are in balance - can only be achieved through the founder or founders letting go of their charismatic influence and their instinctive need to control everything that moves, towards allowing the ever-complex business to evolve a degree of systematic regulation. Several of the coaching associations have successfully navigated the founder's dilemma (not always bloodlessly, but the transition traversed nonetheless), often leaving the founder casting a patrician eye over proceedings from a detached position. By contrast, there remain examples of other associations that, far from navigating the founder's dilemma, have not even turned to face it, with the founders remaining in a position of high control. So far, such leaders have shown no signs of ever stepping aside. In one example, even after two decades, there is no evidence of a succession strategy, and surprisingly, there is little evidence of challenge from members regarding this continuous wielding of almost dynastic power presented as benevolence, the founder remained in place.

In one form or another, each of these associations have adopted some form of recognisable governance to adapt to the demands of the systematisation phase. Some associations have set down books of rules and processes with bureaucratic diligence, in at least one example diligently followed, while other associations, after a flurry of enthusiastic compliance, have maintained the cosmetic patina of an ethics-based structural form, while making moves within those processes that might not have stood up to forensic scrutiny if ever held up to the light. There have been examples of the enthusiastic setting up of democratic fora such as AGMs at the pioneering stage, only for them to fall into disrepair, while high-sounding ethics policies and codes of conduct, painstakingly crafted and then announced amid much fanfare, are subsequently rarely pulled off the shelf. Meanwhile, in the persistent absence of external regulation, more and more sophisticated iterations of 'pseudo-regulation' have been paraded, but with few examples of robust enforcement.

Several of these associations have designed processes for leadership election and succession which define time-limits for these officers' periods in office, put in place to safeguard against dynasties forming. While some associations have been scrupulous in ensuring this refreshment of the leadership group occurs, others have allowed this to slide, especially when among the leadership there reside individuals who carry much of the administrative donkey work and who prove themselves indispensable. Retaining hold of the bureaucratic reins and the rule-making formulation has brought considerable power behind the scenes to these individuals, sometimes operating in the organisations' shadows, exerting Rasputin type skills in political manoeuvring. In most associations, some form of second chamber existed in terms of an independent Boards of Governors - whose role it was to hold the executive to account, and to mediate between members and executive – was inaugurated. It is difficult to generalise across the associations as to the efficacy of these second chambers, though there are examples where governors folded all too easily when pushed back on by the executive, neatly enacting a reflexive defensive routine that maintains the status quo.

In the struggle to maintain harmonic functioning, most of these associations have suffered power struggles and behind the scenes epic battles, but these conflicts have rarely been played out in front of the infantilised members. Inevitable conflicts of interest have bubbled to the surface from time to time, especially where association executives have also held directorial roles within satellited training and assessment provider companies. When push came to shove, their allegiance proved to be more or less towards their commercial loyalties rather than the greater good of the association.

During the maturation phase, some of these institutions have practised financial transparency and accountability to their members, while for others the financial performance of the association has remained obscure to lay members. In some instances, this has been aided by the fact their 'limited by association' constitution has not required them to disclose more than a basic balance sheet, without even the requirement for audit. While some activists and dissidents among the membership have, from time to time, pushed for financial accountability, for most lay members that disaffection rarely rises above a low-grade grumble. These passive members are content that they maintain their badge, and do not have the stamina to push for challenge of internal processes, priorities, or fealties. If leaders are unseated, then it is more often through internal putsch than an upsurge of democratic protest.

The main operational engine for each of the associations remained the continuous throughput of volunteers who have sedulously and often selflessly kept the show on the road, although the volume and complexity of demand that systematisation ushered in meant that full-time employees needed to be employed, not only to deal with the volume of incoming traffic but also to exercise imported professional expertise. There are also many examples of volunteers in hybridised semi-employed roles; some of which have grown to the extent that the volunteer in question has graduated to the status of virtual full-time employee, where that role has become an important part of their personal identity. In many cases such individuals carry significant 'organisational memory,' providing operational continuation as titular leaders and executives have come and gone. There have existed many predictable tensions between the centrally based executives who dictate policy and those long-suffering volunteers who are required to enact these policies at ground level. Such tensions have been exacerbated while the leaders are seen to be enjoying fine dinners and free conference invites, while the volunteers labour away in the backroom, struggling to figure out how to pay for all the policies they seek to enact.

During this late maturation phase, especially as home markets became supersaturated, the associations sought to colonise new geographies, or to combine with equivalent associations within these new geographies. These colonial manoeuvres in turn demanded additional levels and forms of governance. Most of these associations adopted a federal model, with some exhibiting a degree of negotiable subsidiarity between the centre and federal entities, while others elected for higher degrees of central control. There is evidence that, in early stages of colonisation - during the metaphorical exchanging of furs for tobacco and beads - or of new members for a signifier of professional identity - the ceding of power to the centre was warmly welcomed. However, as the federations matured, the challenges made to the paternalistic and sometimes condescending centre increased, but rarely to the extent of displacing the centre.

This headlong charge for global growth – and bragging rights to the same - ushered in all the worst characteristics of hyper competition, with all parties engaged in a spiralling numbers game including ticking off numbers of territories, numbers of members, numbers of products on offer. Attempts were made to form fine-sounding global alliances, but these proved to be short lived. Efforts to consolidate and augment various offerings in line with self-regulation were posited and trialled, but these ran into deep cultural impediments to merging offerings in the face of competitive imperatives. English remained the main means of communication, which meant that power and control over the shaping of the profession, to a great extent, remained with the Western hemisphere centres in the USA, UK, Paris and Brussels. There is an argument that the drive for global dominance deepened tendencies towards the infantilisation of the membership, and the encouragement of construction of messiah figures, mainly male celebrity coaches, who were awarded fully funded ambassadorships to proselytise the word according to their sponsoring association.

Advances in technology had an undoubted impact on the maturity phase of these associations, bringing with it its own challenges and dilemmas, not least in the cost of setting up and then maintaining sophisticated web platforms that often proved less than user-friendly to members with basic information needs. While the use of Zoom and equivalent technologies enabled much more frequent exchange than was possible in the past between the organisations and its peoples, it also foreshadowed a growing personal distance between leaders and members as in-person limited informal exchanges became more limited, consolidating formal power distance.

In the face of this distancing, what members talked most warmly of was opportunities for embodied face-to-face sharing between members at localised network meetings and national training and education events, circling back to the original impetus for personal connection that drove the creation of the associations in their earliest pioneering days. Technology capability unleashed a bombardment of product offerings, emailed to all members on a weekly basis, that proved attractive to some but deeply irritating to others, especially when most of these offerings had a price tag attached. This sense of aggravation was intensified when these offers were being made at the point when many coaches were on squeezed incomes, and already feeling betrayed by the false promises sold to them by the associations and their training providers of the commercial sunny uploads promised once the prospective clients caught sight of the newly anointed member's shiny credentials.

Colonisation Strategies: An Ethical Analysis

In the ever-evolving world of coaching, coaching associations are constantly seeking new avenues for growth and expansion. To achieve this, they often look beyond saturated domestic markets and instead focus on opening up new fields by employing colonisation strategies, as they move into new territories, which exporting their coaching models, philosophies, and practices to foreign territories.

An interesting aspect of these colonisation strategies is the resemblance they bear to the tactics employed by earlier religions and cults. It is important to clarify that this parallel does not imply that coaching association are religions or cults themselves. However, the similar approach lies in the practices of sending 'ambassadors' with self-proclaimed credentials to anoint new recruits, thereby spreading the influence of the coaching association. The ethical implications of sending self-proclaimed 'ambassadors' to anoint novices in the coaching domain remains a concern, as it continues to happen. While these ambassadors may possess extensive coaching experience and knowledge, the validity of their self-proclaimed credentials to a different culture and geography can be called into question. This raises concerns about transparency, credibility, and the exploitation of vulnerable individuals seeking personal and professional growth. This exploitation can include financial costs, false promises, or misguiding individuals into adopting specific coaching practices without proper validation.

Similar to the tactics employed by religious sects, coaching association often use persuasive techniques to create a sense of dependency among their followers. By positioning themselves as the ultimate source of answers and solutions, coaching association tap into the desires of naive individuals seeking guidance. This creates a power dynamic that can be exploitative and raises ethical concerns. Coaching associations, in their zeal to colonise, often omit to prioritise informed consent, by way of ensuring that potential members are fully aware of the coaching process, its limitations, and potential benefits. The use of colonisation strategies that play on the desires of individuals seeking answers may obscure the true nature of coaching, potentially leading to unintended consequences or dependency on the coaching association itself.

As coaching association employ tactics reminiscent of earlier religions and cults, they may tap into the desires of individuals seeking answers, security through the promotion of a celebrity coach not only as their ambassador, but also as a messiah-like figure. The desire for personal growth, self-discovery, and a greater purpose can create vulnerability in individuals, making them susceptible to undue influence and manipulation.

While the expansion of coaching association into new territories is a natural consequence of market saturation, it is essential to examine the ethical implications of employing strategies reminiscent of earlier religions and cults. By respecting informed consent, practicing transparency, and prioritising accountability, coaching association can ensure they are providing genuine guidance while safeguarding against the exploitation of vulnerable individuals. As the coaching industry continues to evolve, maintaining ethical standards should remain a top priority, ensuring that the pursuit of growth does not compromise the principles that underpin coaching as a beneficial practice.

Follow the money – pulling back the curtain

It is often said that for any serious investigation to get to the core of what may lie behind a series of shadowy occurrences that cause concern within an organisation, then the advice is 'to follow the money.' In the case of coaching associations, this is easier said than done – not impossible, but in most cases, it takes effort, which most often lead to a dead end. While it is difficult to generalise across the associations, one observation would be that while in the early pioneering days the finances were transparent, for all members to see and argued over; delivered through annual accounts at AGMs and the likes; that as time went on and the associations moved into maturity phase, then the degree of transparency lessened, perhaps benignly explained by the increasing organisational and commercial complexity that accompanies growth; or more controversially explained by a wish to keep the finances obscure.

To this day, the most financially transparent of the associations remains the ICF, whose full balance sheet and Profit and Loss statements are in the public domain, for all to scrutinise. Given that the ICF boasts 50,000 members, including life coaches as well as those working in the organisational domain, then the figures probably eclipse the revenues of all of the other associations put together, though that statement is speculative, as no other associations shows the same public transparency. For year 2019, the ICF total assets stand at $17,183,976.

Looking at the ICF revenue line for 2019, then the following is revealed.

Memberships - $7,696, 970
Credentialing - $3,200, 522.
Programs   - $962, 940

On the costs side

Membership- $871,737
Credentialing - $911, 078
Management fees - $4,663,031.

These figures speak to the ICF being a significant market player by any definition of the same, and the ratios between membership and credentialing worthy of note, should one ever be in doubt as to whether credentialing comprises a significant revenue stream, even a 'cash cow.'

While USA accounting protocols require this level of disclosure, the same does not apply to those associations domiciled in the UK for accounting purposes. In fact, both the

EMCC UK and the Association for Coaching (AC) remind us that, as companies 'limited by association,' they are not obliged to reveal audit. All that is out there in the public domain, then, is that,

EMCC UK – 2022 – reserves of £257, 671. Requests for P&L denied.
AC net assets – 2022 - £589,476. (unaudited) Requests for P&L denied.
AC international (same directors as AC) £334,962 (unaudited) Requests for P&L denied.
APECS – 2022 net assets - £53,507 (unaudited) APECS – Association for Professional and Executive Coaching and Supervision.

As far as can be discerned, none of the above associations websites refers to financing or accounting details to their members. When EMCC and AC have repeatedly been asked for details of P&L, the response has been that all they are obliged to share is what can be seen on Companies House. As for EMCC Global, the central entity of EMCC, based in Belgium, through which its various national affiliates are satellited, the same answer is given – that they are not obligated to reveal any accounts, even to members. It is difficult to navigate a way through Belgium Company registrations to find a set of accounts. These refusals compound the 'fatal flaw' regarding the lack of external regulation that would demand accountability from these entities.

In the case of these European associations then, the pattern of refusal to disclose the monies is striking, given that in the early days such figures were open to all members. What is known though, is the through virtual ownership and control, that the appointed directors exert significant power over the allocation of their funds. A deeper exploration of Companies House data reveals a rather alarming churn of directors within the EMCC over the past ten years, not least in the position of President. This high turnover rate of those in positions of power would beg the question as to whether these funds were under secure stewardship.

The AC and AC International, by contrast, have had the same three directors since their inception in 2002. Last year, one of these directors died, leaving the same two directors in control of all fund dispersal, and residing over significant cash in hand that grows year on year.

In conclusion regarding 'following the money,' then the ICF is highly transparent. It does serve as a reminder that it is possible for coaching associations can be big business, and can generate significant revenues, not least through credentialing. While it cannot be assumed that the fees-to-credentials ratio for ICF applies to other associations; then it is fair to assume that the growth in accreditation offerings across all the associations is not purely driven by altruistic motives to drive up professional standards. The constitutional choice of 'company be association, limited by guarantee,' allows these association to refuse scrutiny with impunity.

Facing squeezes on coaches' discretionary spend.

For some considerable time, the market for executive and life coaching has been supersaturated by an over-supply of providers, both accredited and those without recognised credentials. At the same time, over the past twenty-five years, there has been a corresponding growth in the number of coaching associations seeking to meet the professional needs of these coaches. Bob Garvey suggests that the 'wild west of coaching' – which we were all warned of in 2012, has been replaced by a 'wild west of coaching associations,' each competing in their own saturated market. Given the downturn in world economies, and growing sophistication of coaching buyers, and relative price inelasticity, then it could well be that, when a significant number of coaches, wishing some form of legitimation, will sign up for association membership and education, they will tend to go for lower price, lower barrier to entry options; or none at all, as they gain confidence in their own ability to do good business without credentials.

 Just as the buyers for coaching have grown more sophisticated; so too have the buyers of coaching associations and providers. The effect of this in a saturated market of competing associations could well be to drive associations to lower price and lower standards, to remain in business, or to be tempted by the economies to be gained through digitalisation. Such a lowering of standards and vigilance could well, over time, lead to the discrediting of the 'profession' as a whole. A worst case, then could well be that the market for one-size fits all coaching education implodes, taking with it the unitary coaching associations who are reliant on uniform delivery in an unregulated market.

The commercial growth imperative, which refers to the pressure for constant economic growth and profit maximisation, can potentially corrupt the executive coaching industry in many ways, such as misaligned focus, where coaches and their associations prioritising quick fixes and superficial solutions, rather than addressing deeper issues and fostering long-term growth and development for their clients. Allied to that is the temptation to oversell, over promise and underdeliver, resulting in disappointment when clients do not achieve immediate or miraculous results. In extreme cases, it can even result in unethical practices, such as making false claims about the outcomes or benefits of coaching. Then there is the increased focus on selling pre-packaged coaching programs or one-size-fits-all approaches rather than tailoring coaching to the unique needs and circumstances of individual clients. This in turn fosters credential inflation, where the emphasis on certifications and credentials is sought by coaching associations and their tethered providers to differentiate themselves and attract clients.

There is little doubt that coaching associations move when the market moves, though not necessary at the same time, due to a lag created by cumbersome bureaucratic processes. If coaches are feeling market pressure, then so too will their satellited associations, who themselves can find themselves in a hyper-competitive market with their counterpart associations. This may in turn drive them to misaligned focus, quick fixes, over-selling, over-promising, credential dilution, increasing standardisation, and the lowering of scrutiny of members claims for credentials and experience.

Opportunity Cost impact causing coaches to abandon ship

Many coaches choose to join a coaching association for the purposes of accessing a platform for networking, continuing education, and recognition within the industry. However, the cost associated with membership in these coaching association has become a pertinent issue, raising the question of whether exorbitant membership fees drive coaches away. Membership fee rates in coaching associations are often structured to cover expenses related to administrative costs, infrastructure, professional development opportunities, and maintaining the organisation's reputation and credibility. Additionally, being a part of these association may also provide coaches with access to networking events and resources aimed at fostering professional growth. While these benefits are indeed valuable, it is important to assess whether the financial burden incurred by coaches seeking membership outweighs the advantages offered.

For coaches who are just starting out on their careers or working in a less financially abundant region, high membership costs can pose a significant impediment.

Considering that some coaching association charge significant annual fees, coaches may struggle to allocate such a substantial sum from their limited earnings. This creates a dilemma for coaches between investing in their professional growth or trying to stabilise their own financial situation. Consequently, many aspiring coaches who drop out in the face of these financial demands may find themselves excluded from opportunities for networking and further education, hindering their professional development progress.

Moreover, even experienced coaches might eventually reach a threshold where the cost of maintaining multiple coaching association memberships becomes economically unviable. With multiple associations focusing on various niches or specialisations, coaches often face the decision of selecting which coaching association to join based on their financial feasibility. However, this not only limits their exposure to different coaching perspectives but may also lead to divisions in the coaching community.

Membership fees for coaching association vary significantly based on the organisation and the level of membership chosen. While some coaches may view the cost as an investment in their career development, others may find it to be a financial burden. As coaches often operate as independent professionals, funding membership fees entirely out of their own pocket can become challenging, particularly for those just starting or operating in lower-income settings. When the cost of membership overshadows the perceived benefits, coaches may be driven away, especially if they feel they can access similar resources and learning opportunities elsewhere.

Moreover, some coaching associations impose ongoing renewal fees, which can add to the financial strain experienced by coaches. These fees are intended to cover administrative costs, maintain the association's infrastructure, and ensure ongoing support for members. However, if coaches find that the benefits offered by the organisation do not justify the perpetual financial obligations, they may choose to discontinue their membership. This decision may be further compounded if coaches believe that the resources and opportunities made available to them can be acquired through alternative means, such as attending independent workshops or seeking online learning platforms.

In addition to membership and renewal fees, coaches may also encounter additional expenses related to mandatory certifications or accreditations required by coaching bodies. While these requirements are often seen as a means of consolidating professionalism, competence, and ethical practices within the coaching industry, the associated costs can be a significant barrier for coaches who are unable to meet these financial obligations. This may lead coaches to question whether the benefits derived from these certifications outweigh the financial burden, potentially driving them away from the coaching association altogether.

A deeper consideration lies in the fact that coaches also need to evaluate the return on investment from their membership within coaching bodies. If coaches do not see a tangible return in terms of increased credibility, networking opportunities, or access to a wider client base, they may question the value they receive for their membership fees. In this scenario, coaches might opt to redirect their financial resources towards other avenues that offer a greater return on investment or allocate their time and effort to building their personal brand independently.

It is important to recognise that the decision to withdraw membership from a coaching association due to cost is subjective and highly dependent on the individual coach's circumstances, financial resources, and perception of value. What may be expensive for one coach could be perceived as affordable for another, depending on their financial standing and goals. It may well be that for those most in need of building networks and skills, then membership of an association may be unaffordable; while for those with a mature reputation and customer base, then membership is no longer a necessary cost of doing business, whether affordable or not.

Early Decline and Fragmentation Stage

As world shifted its attention, in the 2010s and beyond, towards the pressing global crises regarding climate and the North South divide, and inequalities of gender, race, and income, the coaching associations pivoted to align themselves with efforts to address these global crises, partly because they felt it was morally the right thing to do, but also, one might suggest, to appear awake and relevant. The motivation for this switch seemed mixed, entangled. Each association set up their own working parties to figure how coaching might contribute to averting disaster. Most of the proposed solutions centred on the education and influencing of their clients to become more aware of environmental and social responsibilities within their own ecosystems. This press for outward focus was overlain with the coaching world aligning with the need for personal wellness and spiritually based practices to combat the exigencies and uncertainties that were assaulting their clients in a VUCA (Volatility, Uncertainty, Complexity, and Ambiguity) world.

While these efforts were all very commendable, and hard to argue against without seeming uncaring, many members questioned how this shrill insistence on coaching freighting global transformation agendas would be preferable to the simpler paradigm of sitting with the client and working with them on what comes up – the mantra of 'start where the client is at.' These sceptics struggled to recognise themselves within these pushes for legitimation, for relevance, even wondering if it was an attempt to divert attention away from the fact that the old order of selling membership and credentials was no longer capturing the imagination of existing or prospective clients. Were global crises just something else to talk about, a deflection, while the traditional selling continued unabated, revealing the Janus face of late modern coaching associations?

Accreditations, like the poor, remained with us through all of this, but metastasised from the original model of one or two basic accreditation offerings from each association towards in some cases ten or twelve complex products. These often-overlapping credentials, labelled with undecipherable acronyms that only the respective associations' cognoscenti would understand or value, tumbled onto the market at precipitous speed. On top of that, it transpired that each of these newly unveiled competencies would require supervision, which in turn meant the creation of yet more supervision accreditations also. These accreditations were, more often than not, trialled by officers of the associations, who were among the first to be awarded such. Some members were keen to be first movers in the collecting of these shiny new badges, while others were growing weary, cynical of this bombardment of accreditations, labelling them a racket.

There is evidence that technological contagion, contemporary crises of purpose and identity and supersaturation of mature markets were all symptoms of these associations entering the 'decline' stage of their organisation lifecycles. One characteristic of the decline stage is the rise of an aristocracy, who enjoy the allure of privileges, indulge in favouritism, and exploit opportunities for personal gain, acquired through pecuniary or other less tangible currencies. In the coaching landscape, one phenomenon reflective of this decline phase was the creation of WEBECS, 'The World Business & Executive Coach Summit,' which claims it is the place "where the future goes to be born." WEBECS is a different type of coaching association, where it gathers together coaching 'thought leaders', digitally, on an annual basis, for the rest of the coaching world to learn from through masterclasses, and through orchestrated debates which rarely become contentious, alongside more straightforward expositions of their resident gurus' ideologies and practices, all conducted in the spirit of glowing positivity and mutual appreciation.

A further manifestation of the aristocracy stage would be the instance where three venerable British celebrity coaches, now in their seventies and in many ways lifelong commercial competitors who each had played prominent leadership roles within and across coaching associations, chose to come together to offer their collective wisdom on 'team coaching'. Team coaching was one of the latest products in the executive coaching shop window, presented to the market as a natural extension of one-on-one coaching, as if it were a freshly mined discovery. In fact, it proved to be little other than the rebadging of long-established Organisation Development practice, where these luminaires had cut their professional teeth in the first place. There was a cleverness in this sleight of hand, where these dynastic leaders laying down arms to come together for one last gig helped maintain the hegemony of the aristocracy, reminding neophytes of their place in history.

A further classical manifestation of the decline stage was that, in the face of such aristocratic showboating, a groundswell of cynicism and disillusionment was festering among journeymen coaches towards the old order and their attempts to renew their market offerings alongside renewing their relevance. Noticing this vulnerability - these cracks in the carapace of the established order - previous outliers and niche players entered the association game, some claiming to be avant-garde, some environmentally action aligned, most claiming to be spiritually awake, all protesting their valorisation of the 'inner being' as much as the 'outer doing,' and to a person claiming to have moved away from the twentieth century paternalistic structures that underpin the traditional coaching associations. These emergent, networked associations were (and mostly still are) messiah led, their impulse evangelical, embracing a new world order that leans on systemic thinking and distributed leadership, and healing of past injustices.

Somewhat ironically, but perhaps inevitably, these new order associations, in their developmental trajectories, have begun to reflect 'path dependency' towards manifesting the artefacts of the old order that they stated it was their purpose to usurp. Examples of such mirroring of older forms would include their claiming common cause with alternative thought leaders – alternative in their philosophies, sure enough, but celebrities in their own right all the same. The semiotics of naming of such associations is telling; a call-back to the past, in examples such as David Drake's 'The Moment Institute,' Simon Western's 'Eco-leadership Institute,' Otto Scharmer's 'Presencing Institute.' Institutional theorists would have a field day in the deconstruction of these social constructions, as they seek legitimation and permanency in a suggestible and contested landscape.

While these newly formed 'institutes' first found their feet and sense of momentum through the offering of radically alternative experimental workshops and associated writings, as their confidence grew they moved away from these originally edgy workshops towards regurgitating the same ideas but in commodified form, and at a high end price point. The next step beyond that was to further monetise their networks through offering levels of accreditation to those who wished to sit at their feet, and then practice in their image and likeness, with their imprimatur duly stamped.

Emergent technologies such as Zoom, LinkedIn, Twitter (X), the blogosphere and podcasting created channels for massified broadcasting of their teachings and philosophies from a low-cost base. Happy to morph into alternative 'content providers,' they relied nonetheless on a devoted volunteer base to drive their operational engine, echoing the resourcing pattern of their much-maligned traditional predecessors. There is evidence from their publicity materials that these latter-day messiahs felt that, in their hubristic driving of their distinctive cultures, they had all of their followers with them, attracted mainly not only by their individual charisma but also by the rightness and justice of their cause. In reality, such devotion was not universally the case. The cold fact was that quite a number of their customers signed up for their accreditations and workshops largely because they felt the need for a licence to operate of some kind. They decided that one of these funkier badges would serve as well as a traditional award, while offering them a more provocative way of looking at the world. It also allowed them to make claim to alternative contemporary practice, rather than identifying with traditional associations and their accreditations that were growing old in the eyes of the market, and furthermore were growing saturated on the supply side, with so many already holding those two-a-penny awards.

Many of these emergent associations emphasised as their point of difference a premium on 'reflective practice' as a necessary feature of both coach and client development. Traditional associations were not slow to echo the need for reflective practice, with many of them asking for evidence of written reflective practice portfolios as one element of their accreditation submissions. Indeed, when asked, students who had completed such portfolios attested to the deep learning they had gained from such reflective writing. However, the same students doubted whether reflection was truly valorised by the awarding associations, given the quiet space it needed, and its requirement for the allowing of unknowing. There was a feeling that deep reflective practice was fighting a losing battle in the face of the temptation for coaches on their learning curve to assimilate fresh developmental 'content' which appealed to the increasingly short attention-span zeitgeist, delivering dopamine spikes on a regular basis, rather than the slow burn that reflective practice brings.

Respectable qualitative research has highlighted the contribution that reflective practice made to coaching efficacy but these findings were competing for shelf space among the more instant solutions that offered immediate uplift of practice and the ubiquitous 'unlocking of potential.' Meanwhile Business Schools were increasingly entangled in their own psychodramas with regard to being at the forefront of the marketisation imperative that had seized universities worldwide. Some business schools who focussed on coaching theory and practice maintained a degree of academic freedom and integrity with regard to the coaching phenomenon, while others piled in to capitalise on alliances and mergers with coaching associations, providers, and their attendant celebrities, hand in hand, in symbiotic union. Independent research was becoming mired in a swamp of solution offering studies that were studded with confirmation bias, while attempts to prove 'return on investment' directly attributable to coaching interventions grew weaker by the day. To their credit, where universities offer in-house accredited degrees, they have displayed levels of rigour and regulation well beyond those administered by the associations, with some honourable exceptions.

Alongside of this mixed economy of established associations and the emergent new wave, both based on a similar business model where growth is the implicit imperative, there has arisen a quite different emancipatory wave espousing the value of 'coaching for everyone,' not just for the few who could most afford it but least needed it, compared to those struggling on the edges of society. These efforts, based on Artificial Intelligence technology, promise massified coaching on a huge scale, reaching out via smart phones to those struggling and deeply in need of support and guidance.

Should such a push prove successful, it would fundamentally undermine the old order of coaching, deeply challenging its power structures and basic assumptions. While many coaches are emotionally and philosophically inclined to support this emancipatory drive, they are also apprehensive as to its impacts on their own business models and fee structures. At less emancipatory level, but still AI based and massified, are commercially based new entrants such as Better Up which offer much lower cost life coaching to a wide market whose lives are lived on the web.

Challenges to the volunteer defence

When members of professional coaching associations find themselves dissatisfied with the levels of service or lacking value in the products they receive, it is disheartening to find that they face a common defensive wall: the 'volunteer defence.' While many coaching associations are resourced by volunteers who genuinely strive to elevate the coaching profession, it is all the more important to scrutinise how this defence is articulated.

Coaching associations argue that their volunteers (including their leaders often!), give their dedication and commitment for nothing, therefore it is unkind to challenge their performance. They emphasise the idea of selflessly contributing to the development and regulation of the coaching industry. One of the primary aspects of the volunteer defence centres around the lack of financial compensation for the work performed. Volunteers cannot be pushed further. Amateur enthusiasts they may be, but they are doing their best - you must forgive their mistakes, lest they leave.

They argue that limited time availability often prevents them from allocating enough resources to address every concern or improve the quality of service and value perceived by their members. Coaching associations often stress that their volunteers are driven by a deep passion for the coaching profession, and their commitment is an act of goodwill.

Professional coaching associations frequently claim that their limited resources are the main reason behind any shortcomings in service or value. They assert that without adequate funding, staffing, and technological capabilities, they are unable to provide an optimal level of service to their members. However, by adopting this defence, coaching associations risk undermining their credibility by suggesting that their operations are not sustainable or effectively managed.

Such associations assert that their existence revolves around the significance of collective effort. They stress that it takes the involvement and collaboration of all members to build and improve the coaching industry. By asserting the importance of unity, coaching associations attempt to divert attention from their shortcomings and instead focus on fostering a sense of collective responsibility. However, this objection may not provide a compelling defence if the service or product value provided by the coaching association fails to meet the basic expectations of their members.

While coaching associations often hire professionals to support volunteers in essential services like payment collection and marketing, they continue to assert the significant advantages that the volunteer defence offer. They argue that volunteers bring a unique blend of passion, dedication, and genuine interest to the table. Their deep knowledge of the organisation's values and goals often surpasses that of paid professionals, making them ideal brand ambassadors, which can compensate for their lack of formal training.

Unlike paid staff, volunteers willingly offer their time and energy, often driven by personal connections to the cause or organisation. The intrinsic motivation of volunteers fosters a strong commitment, ultimately leading to reliable and consistent performance.

Opponents argue that volunteers may not always be available or accessible due to personal obligations or conflicting commitments. Conversely, professionals hired specifically for payment collection and marketing can ensure 24/7 availability. While this objection may hold some truth, volunteer defence has the potential to counterbalance this drawback through effective scheduling, clear communication channels, and a larger volunteer pool. By having a robust structure in place and ensuring adequate coverage through volunteer recruitment, they argue that associations can mitigate any constraints imposed by limited availability.

Critics often claim that volunteers lack the accountability necessary for essential services like payment collection and marketing. The fear of potential negligence or mishandling of funds can be a cause for concern. However, coaching associations often assert that a volunteer basis offers inherent advantages in terms of accountability. Volunteers operate with a sense of personal responsibility and pride, aware that their actions reflect on the organisation as a whole.

Volunteers struggles in the face of digitalisation of member services.

In the realm of technology-driven businesses, the role of algorithms has become increasingly crucial. With their ability to optimise operations, adapt in real-time, and predict future outcomes, algorithms have revolutionised various industries. However, it can be asserted that although volunteerism has its merits, it cannot replicate the same level of understanding and deployment of algorithms as specialised IT professionals.

The domain of algorithms is constantly evolving, driven by advancements in technology and data analysis techniques. IT professionals dedicate their careers to researching, studying, and adapting to these advancements, ensuring their knowledge base remains up-to-date. Conversely, volunteers typically engage in short-term commitments, often focusing on areas unrelated to algorithmic development. Therefore, they may lack the time, motivation, or resources to acquire the necessary expertise to deeply understand and deploy algorithms used in business operations. Ethical issues like algorithmic bias, privacy concerns, and fairness require careful consideration throughout the algorithmic development and deployment lifecycle. IT professionals comprehend these nuances and can architect algorithms that uphold ethical standards. Volunteers, well-intentioned as they may be, may overlook or not fully grasp the potential ethical challenges associated with algorithmic decision-making within a business context.

When volunteers protest that they are quite able to understand and use algorithms within coaching associations, they may be bypassing the inherent accountability that should accompany such powerful tools. This lack of accountability hampers the ability to identify and rectify errors, leading to ineffective or biased decision-making. Consequently, members may suffer from unsatisfactory outcomes or unfair treatment due to the inability to challenge the system effectively. Without adequate knowledge of the underlying mechanisms, there is an increased risk of biases being embedded within the algorithms, leading to potentially discriminatory practices. This can perpetuate existing inequalities and impede the association's efforts to promote fairness and inclusivity.

Effectively implementing algorithms requires continuous evaluation, improvement, and adaptation to remain efficient and relevant. By deploying algorithms without understanding, volunteers hinder the potential for innovation and progress within the coaching association. The inability to comprehend and make necessary adjustments limits the association's ability to adapt to emerging trends and address evolving member needs effectively.

Volunteers who deploy algorithms without thorough comprehension inadvertently place themselves and coaching associations at risk of exploitation. Malicious actors can exploit algorithmic weaknesses, potentially resulting in data breaches, privacy violations, or manipulation of learning experiences. Without a sound grasp of the algorithms' inner workings, volunteers may struggle to identify potential vulnerabilities, thereby inadvertently leaving learners exposed to various threats

Algorithms serve as the backbone of coaching associations' competency grid-based systems, facilitating assessment and feedback mechanisms based on such girds. However, when volunteers lack the necessary insights into these algorithms, they run the risk of perpetuating biased or inconsistent evaluations. This imbalance can result in incorrect assessments of coaching competencies and consequently hinder the effectiveness of learning and accreditation services. The dissemination of inaccurate feedback can severely undermine the progress and growth of coaches, impeding their potential to achieve their full capabilities, and reflect badly on the associations prompting such competency grids.

In conclusion, the dangers of deploying algorithms without understanding them are substantial, particularly when applied to learning and accreditation services within coaching associations. From perpetuating biases and propagating inaccurate outcomes to compromising privacy and eroding human connection, the implications of uninformed algorithm deployment are far-reaching and concerning. Addressing these dangers necessitates providing volunteers with the necessary knowledge and training to make informed decisions, ensuring algorithms are developed with checks and balances, and placing continued emphasis on the importance of human judgement and compassion in coaching associations. Failure to address these concerns may compromise the integrity, fairness, and effectiveness of coaching associations, leaving learners vulnerable and impeding their growth in meaningful ways.

Espoused ethics and ethics in practice

The perceived gap between the values publicly expressed by these coaching associations and the values enacted in practice is a cause for concern. While coaching associations often articulate high ethical standards, instances of unethical behaviour can still be found. This inconsistency suggests that the perceived values upheld by coaching associations are not consistently enforced. The lack of coherence between what is claimed and what is practiced raises concerns about the integrity and credibility of these organisations.

One indication that coaching associations prioritise espoused values is their failure to address systemic issues, rather than simply addressing transgressions on a case-by-case basis. Associated with this avoidance of systemic issues is coaching associations limited accountability and transparency regarding the adherence to claimed values. Often, there is minimal public disclosure of actions taken to address deviations from espoused values. This opacity allows coaching associations to prioritise their reputation over true accountability. Without robust mechanisms and public scrutiny, and enforcement of disciplinary measures, coaching associations could exploit the gap between espoused and performed values to carry out actions that contradict their stated principles. This weak enforcement contributes to a cycle where misconduct among members or officers of becomes acceptable, undermining the reputation and credibility of the coaching associations.

One could argue that the persistence of espoused values in coaching associations is partly due to their resistance to change and adaptation. Traditions and established practices can inhibit the evolution of values in line with contemporary developments. The reluctance to embrace change prevents coaching associations from effectively addressing emerging challenges and failings. This resistance perpetuates a culture where espoused values are sacred rhetoric rather than the driving force behind coaching practices.

The absence of Informed consent while marketing and growing Coaching Associations

Coaching associations should make clear to potential members the possible downsides of joining their organisation. For instance, members, beyond application and enrolment, may feel overwhelmed by the amount of personal work and digging into practice records required in applying for accreditation. More profoundly, it needs to be made clear that coaching often involves delving into deep-rooted beliefs and patterns, which can be emotionally challenging. Additionally, individuals may experience frustration or disappointment if they do not see immediate progress in their personal or professional lives.

Failure to seek informed consent by not outlining these limitations and downsides can feed false hopes. Potential members or newbies may have unrealistic expectations about what coaching associations can provide and believe that membership alone will solve all their problems. This can lead to disappointment and a sense of being misled, hindering their overall experience, and potentially damaging their trust in coaching as a whole. Not providing this information upfront could be seen as an ethical violation by coaching association leadership. It is essential for coaching associations to be transparent and genuine in their approach to potential members. By failing to disclose limitations and downsides, these organisations risk misrepresenting their services and potentially exploiting individuals who are seeking personal growth and support.

When coaching association leaders do not holding their own accreditations.

When the very individuals responsible for selling accreditation do not possess their own accreditations, as has been the case for several European associations, then a worrying scenario unfolds. In such a case, questions regarding transparency and credibility come to the forefront. When candidates who seek accreditation should, by chance, discover the executive's lack of accreditation, it is reasonable for them to demand an explanation for this lack, given the associations' marketing avowals of the many benefits of being credentialled. If the leadership choose not to disclose the reasons for this, then they raise questions that may erode the trust of those seeking accreditation and diminish the transparency expected from a reputable coaching association.

The leadership's assertions that they did not make accreditation a requirement for membership, or that there was no obligation for them to disclose their own lack of accreditation, is a dubious defence that fails to address the concerns raised.

This lack of transparency in not disclosing their own non-accreditation runs in the face of ignoring the need for informed consent regarding the fact that there is no requirement for any member to be accredited. And truthful marketing might include that disclaimer that not even the directors are accredited.

Accreditation is claimed to represent a set of recognised standards and benchmarks that coaches are expected to meet. Coaches who seek accreditation demonstrate their commitment to professional growth, knowledge, and ethical practice. However, if the executive team fails to possess their own accreditations, it casts doubt on their understanding and adherence to these standards, ultimately compromising the quality and credibility of the association's accreditation process.

The commercial aspects of a coaching association selling accreditation without possessing it themselves raises serious concerns about the organisation's motives and intentions. If the primary goal is profit rather than fostering excellence and upholding professional standards, then the commitment to the development and growth of coaches and the raising of professional standards may be compromised. The lack of accreditation among the executive members of a coaching association can significantly undermine the integrity and credibility of the accreditation process. This is primarily because the executive members are responsible for overseeing and supervising the accreditation process, ensuring its fairness, transparency, and adherence to established standards. How can they fully know what it is that they are asking their members to go through, if they themselves have not made that experiential journey?

Moreover, the lack of accreditation among executive members can also raise doubts about their ability to impartially and fairly assess coaching programs and practitioners. Accreditation processes should be conducted by well-qualified professionals with a broad understanding of coaching practices and a commitment to maintaining high standards. When executive members lack their own accreditation, there may be biases, conflicts of interest, or a lack of understanding of industry norms that could compromise the integrity of the process. Nor are they best qualified to appoint assessors. At a simple level, they open themselves to mockery.

The leadership's failure to pursue accreditation and their subsequent failure to disclose this information also highlights a lack of role modelling and accountability within the coaching association. Executives are expected to set an example for others by demonstrating their commitment to professional growth and adherence to industry standards. By not holding accreditation themselves, the leadership fails to inspire confidence and demonstrate the necessary qualities expected within the coaching profession. The defence that accreditation was not mandatory does little to address the lack of accountability within the executive team.

When candidates discover that the coaching association's leadership lacks accreditation, questions arise regarding potential misrepresentation and misleading claims. Without proper accreditation, the executive team might be improperly positioning themselves as credible authorities in the field. This can lead to false promises and expectations from those who seek their services, impacting both the reputation of the coaching association and the integrity of the accreditation they offer. The defence that accreditation was not required as a standard does not negate the issues of misrepresentation and misleading claims.

The lack of accreditation within the executive leadership of a coaching association. coupled with their failure to disclose this information, raises significant ethical concerns. The defence offered by the leadership, claiming that accreditation is not mandatory, does not adequately address the numerous objections arising from this situation. Breach of trust, lack of role modelling, devaluation of the accreditation, potential misrepresentation, and legal and regulatory implications all undermine the credibility and integrity of the coaching association.

The Burial of Executive Coaches' Metaphorical Dead

When many coaching professionals guide and advise executives – especially those practicing in the performance management field - there remains a concern about the undisclosed mistakes made by executive coaches in the course of their work, amid the suspicion that such mistakes or omissions are seemingly forgotten, buried away from public knowledge..

One possible explanation for the burial of metaphorical dead is rooted in the principle of client confidentiality. Executive coaches are bound by ethical codes that prevent them from publicly disclosing the shortcomings or mistakes of their clients. This confidentiality, while important, raises concerns about the accountability and transparency of executive coaches. By concealing the mistakes made in the course of their client work, or indeed being complicit with ethical misdemeanours committed by the clients themselves, coaches risk perpetuating negative behaviours without holding executives responsible for their actions.

The absence of a standardised framework within the executive coaching industry contributes to the burial of metaphorical dead. While professional associations offer guidelines for executive coaches, there is no robust mechanism to ensure transparency in dealing with their own or clients' mistakes. This lack of standardisation allows executive coaches to handle their failures without proper scrutiny or accountability, making it easier for them to bury their past errors without repercussions.

Executive coaches strive to maintain their reputation and market themselves as experts in their field. Admitting or publicising their mistakes may hinder their ability to secure future clients or tarnish their professional image. Coaches often operates in a results-driven environment, where immediate outcomes are given significant importance. Due to this pressure, coaches may prioritise achieving tangible short-term improvements over addressing deeper, systemic issues. By pushing for quick fixes and not thoroughly examining and addressing their mistakes or poor advice given in the spur of the moment, coaches circumvent the need for long-term solutions. This tendency to overlook underlying problems can lead to the burial of metaphorical dead, as coaches may simply sweep failures under the rug to maintain the illusion of progress.

The absence of a feedback loop within the executive coaching process exacerbates the burial of metaphorical dead. When coaches fail to solicit feedback from their clients regarding the efficacy of their interventions or acknowledge mistakes made, the opportunity for growth and learning diminishes. This lack of feedback perpetuates a cycle where mistakes are ignored, and accountability is eschewed, thereby creating an environment in which errors are conveniently forgotten rather than being addressed and rectified.

Where do coaching associations fit in the scenario of burying the dead? It could be argued in two ways. One would be that while this phenomenon is not covered in codes of conduct, then perhaps it should be. The second inference could be that – if client side mistakes are brushed under the carpet – then the same corrosive principle could apply to the conduct of the associations themselves in the management of their own affairs. For example, in instances where associations have experienced significant leadership disruption, then it might best serve all stakeholders' interests if the underlying reasons for such dislocations were openly shared, rather than be smoothed away or simply buried, never to be mentioned again.

Whistleblowing

While the organisational world in general is embracing the principle of whistle-blowing, and instituting policies that allow a whistle-blower to speak out in relative safety, there is little or no evidence of such policies or even inclination among the coaching associations. The existing codes of ethics point almost exclusively towards member behaviour, not potential transgressions committed by the association itself. There is evidence that when faced with whistleblowing, coaching associations fail to acknowledge their actions, and it pushed, move to threaten or even exclude the whistle-blowers can be challenging, particularly as the whistle-blower has no external regulation to appeal towards.

In extermis, there is evidence that the whistle-blower who persistently challenges the coaching association 's leadership is met with threats of legal action for harassment and defamation. Such actions further exemplify the problematic nature of the coaching association 's practices. Instead of addressing the concerns and rectifying their misconduct, the leadership attempts to silence the whistle-blower, potentially perpetuating a culture of secrecy and suppression. This raises significant ethical questions regarding the organisation's commitment to accountability and transparency.

Ethically, the coaching association is compromised as it loses credibility and fails to uphold the professional standards it claims to champion. Legally, the leadership's threat of legal action against the whistle-blower is concerning, as it seeks to suppress the exposure of their misconduct. The potential legal implications depend on the country or jurisdiction but may include charges of defamation or unfair business practices.

Research – a performative approach?

Coaching associations worldwide have increasingly emphasised their commitment to research in recent years. Some such as the EMCC would claim it has been their USP from their very beginning, This ostensible commitment to research within coaching communities is often displayed through conferences, publications, and collaboration with academic institutions. However, one must question whether this interest is more performative than actual.

It is not to say that coaching association do not engage in any genuine research activities. Some coaching association also publish journals, providing a platform for scholarly work on coaching-related topics. Clearly, there are many benefits of research to the coaching profession, and there is much research into the field occurring quite outside of professional associations. Research, if engaged with, allows coaches to keep up with the latest knowledge and techniques, ensuring their clients receive the best possible support. It provides a foundation for evidence-based practices, promoting credibility and professionalism within the industry. Additionally, research can help identify new avenues for exploration, driving innovation and growth in coaching methods, in addition to promoting continuous self-development within coaches themselves.

Nevertheless, it is crucial to critically evaluate the authenticity and depth of the interest displayed by coaching association in research. Often, the emphasis on research seems to be more performative than actual, aimed at projecting an image of credibility and academic rigor. Coaching organisations may prioritise superficial engagement with research to enhance their reputation, without truly integrating it into the core of their practices, or investing funds into research as a priority, rather then investing funds in research, not relying solely on well meaning early stage researchers. One exception to this this is when they see that faintly disguised market research opportunities could enhance product or service claims.

While coaching associations endorse the importance of research, the actual integration of research findings into coaching techniques may be limited. The gap between academic research and coaching practice remains significant, with many coaches relying on personal experience rather than evidence-based or theory-based approaches. It is remarkable how often associations assert the need to 'bridge the gap' between theory and practice, when they embark on research initiatives. When pressed on association-based practices are research-based, they frequently mention their investment in developing coaching competency grids to support their accreditation programmes. Beyond that, it is hard to indicate where else they claim a research basis for activities, though they will promote many CPD offerings, without necessarily testing the efficacy of such offerings, despite some grandiose claims being made.

There is a tendency to produce simplistic studies or conceptual articles that lack empirical evidence. While such contributions may be valuable in certain contexts, and have strong face validity, they fall short of the rigorous standards set by academic research.

Ultimately, the performative nature of coaching bodies' interest in research becomes evident when we observe the limited impact research has on the profession as a whole. Despite the sheer volume of studies and publications, significant gaps in knowledge and practice persist. Genuine investment in research would involve continuous collaboration with academic institutions and the integration of research into coaching curricula, standards, and guidelines.

Another factor contributing to this performative nature is the pressure to conform to prevailing expectations. In an era increasingly focused on evidence-based decision-making, coaching association may feel obliged to simulate genuine interest in research to maintain relevance and satisfy stakeholders. This outward demonstration can be perceived as a superficial adherence to societal expectations, rather than stemming from an intrinsic passion for knowledge generation and improvement in coaching practices.

While coaching association may claim to prioritise research, several challenges hinder genuine engagement with scholarly inquiry. First, the lack of resources allocated to research initiatives is evident in many coaching organisations. Research requires substantial investments in funding, time, and expertise. Without adequate support, it becomes difficult for coaching association to genuinely engage in research endeavours, limiting their ability to contribute effectively to the field.

Moreover, the practical nature of coaching often creates a tension between research and the immediate demands of clients. Coaching associations generally prioritise the application of methodologies proven effective through practice, such as competency girds, rather than investing time and energy in generating new knowledge. This emphasis on practical outcomes often detracts coaching association from allocating dedicated resources to research, further reinforcing the performative nature of their interest.

It may not be the cost of time and financial investment alone that deters associations from following through on their claims for research commitment more fully. Perhaps there resides an understanding that open-ended research, with no confirmative goal in sight might ask some discomfiting questions not only of the received wisdom of conventional coaching approaches, but also of the underlying assumptions underpinning the need for coaching associations are currently conceived.

It is disheartening to observe that a considerable number of executive coaches exhibit resistance towards engaging with research, with any expressed interest being more apparent than genuine. executive coaching engagements. Sadly, many executive coaches dismiss the significance of research or limit its role to a superficial one, merely using it as a tool to create a façade of credibility or to impress clients.

The resistance to research among executive coaches and their associations may stem from various factors. First and foremost, some coaches might lack the necessary background or training in research methodologies, which they conceive as an activity conducted in an ivory tower by theoreticians without practical experience. As a result, they may feel overwhelmed or perceive research as a time-consuming and complex endeavour. This lack of confidence can manifest as a reluctance to engage with research, choosing instead to rely on their own intuition or experience, which may not always be aligned with the latest management practices or scientific findings.

Furthermore, the pressure to satisfy clients and deliver immediate results within a limited timeframe might contribute to the performative interest in research among coaches. This emphasis on visible outcomes can overshadow the value of thorough depth inquiry, leading coaches to prioritise quick fixes and anecdotal success stories instead. By neglecting research, executive coaches risk conceptualising coaching as a superficial process rather than a deep, introspective journey that yields long-lasting improvement and growth.

.

While there is an expectation that business coaches should read coaching books, this is not always the reality. Time constraints, reliance on practical experience, alternative sources of information, lack of practicality, and rapidly evolving industry trends are all factors that may lead business coaches to prioritize other forms of learning. Ultimately, the decision to read coaching books is likely to vary among different coaches, depending on their individual preferences, priorities, and circumstances.

Do Coaching Associations valorise confirmation data while vigorously suppressing disconfirming information?

Coaching association often have a tendency to valorise confirmation data while suppressing disconfirmative findings, partly out of a desire to maintain a positive reputation. By emphasising positive outcomes and selectively promoting success stories, coaching associations can appear more effective and attract more clients. This tendency to highlight confirmation data not only acts as a marketing strategy but can also serve as a means of maintaining credibility within the industry.

Another reason for coaching associations tendency to focus on confirmation data is because it aligns with their business objectives. These organisations often function as profit-seeking entities, and their primary concern is to secure members and generate revenue. This market-driven approach may lead to the suppression of disconfirmative information, as it does not contribute to the desired image of effectiveness. Coaching associations may have a vested interest in protecting their coaches and their own reputation. If negative feedback or proof of unsuccessful coaching experiences were openly discussed, it could potentially damage the credibility and popularity of the coaching profession as a whole. Therefore, coaching associations tend to adopt a defensive stance, downplaying or even disregarding any disconfirmative findings, ultimately leading to a biased representation of coaching effectiveness.

While executive coaching associations may claim an interest in research, their underlying motivation often lies in market research or product enhancement. These organisations need to create and sell coaching services, and their survival depends on demonstrating the effectiveness and value of their programs. Consequently, the desire to promote their services to potential clients may influence their inclination to embrace and promote confirmation data selectively. By selecting studies that support their particular methodologies, they reinforce the perception that their programs and products are superior to their competitors, and justified investments by prospective members and corporate clients.

The bias towards confirmation data, coupled with the suppression of disconfirmative evidence, within executive coaching association reflects a prioritisation of market research and product enhancement over unbiased research. While this bias may not be intentional, it stems from the need to validate coaching approaches, maintain client confidence, meet expectations, and safeguard professional reputations. To maintain the credibility of executive coaching, it is imperative for coaching association to acknowledge and address this bias, striving for transparency, openness to critical evaluation, and a commitment to evidence-based practices.

However, the exclusive valorisation of confirmation data can have several negative consequences. First, it creates a biased perception of success rates within the field of executive coaching. By only presenting success stories and positive outcomes, these association inflate the impression that coaching is universally effective, which may mislead potential clients into believing that coaching always guarantees positive results. This can lead to unrealistic expectations and disappointment for individuals who do not experience the same level of success.

Moreover, minimising or suppressing disconfirmative information hinders genuine progress and development within the field. Disconfirmative data, such as cases where coaching interventions have not yielded desired outcomes, can offer valuable insights for practitioners to refine their approaches and improve their effectiveness. By neglecting these cases, organisations miss out on opportunities for growth and innovation.

Coaching associations have recognised the allure of promising a high ROI to attract potential members and justify the investment in coaching. Members are naturally drawn to the idea of receiving substantial benefits from their investment, but it is critical to assess the validity of such claims. There is evidence that some coaching providers manipulate data or selectively showcase exceptional cases to bolster the perception of extraordinary results. This cherry-picking approach could create unrealistic expectations for coaches and clients alike. Furthermore, the genuine accomplishments of a few exceptional coaches within a coaching association can inadvertently contribute to the unfounded claims made by others.

One of the main shortcomings in determining the causal basis for coaching companies' ROI claims lies in the scarcity of comprehensive, unbiased research in this field. Many studies have been conducted internally by coaching companies themselves, often leading to a conflict of interest. Isolating the impact of coaching when calculating ROI proves challenging due to the presence of various confounding factors. Factors such as changes in market conditions, competitor activities, or internal policy changes can significantly influence business outcomes and profitability. Neglecting these variables can contribute to exaggerated claims of ROI, thereby undermining the credibility of coaching companies' assertions.

The effectiveness of coaching programs often relies on intangible benefits that are challenging to quantify accurately.

While financial metrics like sales growth or cost reduction are tangible and easily measurable, the impact of coaching on employee motivation, morale, and team dynamics is more subjective and elusive. Failing to adequately measure these intangible benefits can lead to an incomplete assessment of coaching's ROI, potentially exaggerating the claimed figures.

Two-way traffic between Business schools and coaching associations

Over recent years, a trend has emerged where many business schools endorse and accredit the offerings of affiliated coaching companies, even when they are aware of some possibly questionable practices or benefit claims. One driver causing business schools to endorse coaching providers is financial interest, in a the wider context of the wholesale marketisation of universities, with business schools seen as an important cash cow to fuel this commercial drive. Many coaching companies establish partnerships or affiliations with universities, providing these institutions with a substantial revenue stream. This financial dependence can createsan inherent conflict of interest, as the schools may compromise their values and overlook critically evaluating the coaching companies' practices. In such cases, business schools prioritise monetary gains over their duty to provide students with ethical and reputable education and credentialling.

Secondly, the desire to maintain a positive reputation of connection with the 'real world' also influences business schools' endorsement of questionable coaching companies.

By aligning themselves with allegedly prestigious coaching brands, business schools may feel that this enhances their own standing in the eyes of industry. Such affiliations cultivate an illusion of quality and success, leading to increased enrolment and positive perception. Many schools fall into the trap of assuming that affiliated coaching companies are experts solely based on their branding or the reputation of celebrity coaches attached to those providers, while failing to admit their own lack of expertise or experience in the area to do due thorough diligence on such operators.

Furthermore, industry influence and pressure contribute to business schools' endorsement of questionable coaching practices. In an increasingly competitive job market, students are often lured by promises of rapid skill development and guaranteed career success. Coaching companies exploit this demand by offering quick-fix solutions that may lack substantive foundations. Business schools feel compelled to meet these student expectations by endorsing coaching companies that promise immediate results, even if they have not been thoroughly vetted for their efficacy or long-term value. Such pressures can result in postgraduate students passing through the system clutching their certificates, only to find that there is little room for them in an already over-crowded market.

It is worth bearing in mind that not all business school professionals are committed to their institutions or sectors for life. In fact, affiliation with a coaching provider or association can signify an appetising a part time or full-time bridge to an alternative or parallel career path in coaching. One route out of academia can be through academics serving as officers of a coaching association in a monitoring or hands-on capacity. Such roles can serve as a trojan horse into commercial practice.

On the upside, collaboration with coaching providers and associations can create networking opportunities for students, allowing them to connect with established professionals and organisations in the coaching industry. This can lead to internships, mentorships, and job placements, enhancing the students' career prospects. Collaboration can also foster joint research efforts between academia and the coaching industry. This can lead to the generation of new knowledge, best practices, and innovative approaches, further advancing the field of coaching.

However, business schools should carefully assess potential conflicts of interest before collaborating with commercial providers. They should be transparent about any financial arrangements or endorsements that might compromise their impartiality and integrity.

Further, they must maintain control over the design and content of their coaching programs to ensure academic rigor and integrity.

They should critically evaluate the course material provided by commercial providers and ensure it meets the required standards, while ensuring that clear ethical guidelines for their coaching programs are established and ensure that commercial providers also adhere to these standards. Business schools should be transparent with their students, faculty, and stakeholders about any collaborations with commercial providers. Clear disclosure about the nature of the collaboration, financial arrangements, and any potential conflicts of interest is crucial to maintaining trust and integrity.

The emergence of scholar-practitioners on the credentials landscape.

Beyond the borders of coaching 'credential seekers' who rest at the point of having gained an accreditation attesting 'mastery' lie the 'scholar practitioners.' The promotion of this category of scholars is of significant interest to the coaching associations, as they contribute to the legitimation of the associations where it is 'one of their own' who navigates between the professional and the academic ecosystems, producing practice based research that speaks to 'bridging the gap' between practice and theory. W

This category of 'scholar-practitioner' would include those who have stepped out from coaching practice in either a part-time or full-time basis to research an aspect of theirpractice, thereafter to return to practice not only with the satisfaction of having completed an extended piece of intellectual and social inquiry, but also with their studies recognised by the addition of the honorific 'Doctor' or 'Master' on their business card. Many such scholars choose to pursue a 'professional doctorate' rather than a purely academic PhD, where applied learning and action-research approaches that result in recommendations for practice are positively encouraged, rather than a theorised 'contribution to knowledge' alone.

There is no doubt that gaining a professional doctorate also assists in securing part-time of full-time university teaching posts, where the need for a doctorate is increasingly an essential requirement. There is no wish here to downplay the important window that Professional Doctorates play in widening participation in higher education at all levels. However, these awards can be exploited for commercial gain, beyond those unmonetised benefits that which would naturally accrue from hard-earned qualification.

Beyond the intrinsic satisfaction of having brought such a demanded project to fruition – and the gaining of research skills acquired along the way - an increasing number of 'scholar-practitioners' embark upon their studies with the end view of producing a practitioner-friendly 'book', as opposed to a scholarly monograph, clearly in their sights. This newly-minted book will, in the author's eyes at least, present the case for a novel approach to practice, or an extension of professionalisation.

For scholar-practitioners who did not initially embark on their studies with such an end in view, then the realisation that their studies were requiring them to invest in time and money to an extent far beyond anything they had ever anticipated, causes them to wish to capitalize upon and even monetise their considerable investment. The fact that they stumble cross similar practice-based books during the course of their studies helps to crystalize this desire to produce a self-same output.

This practitioner-focused publication, once written, serves not only as an accessible record of their findings but also serves as an elaborate business card (or shelf-ware) to leave behind after client pitches or at subsequent training sessions. The envisioned book can also open doors to conference and seminar invitations from practitioner bodies and business schools alike, in addition to raising their profile within their association. This propensity to publish from research is increasingly encouraged by publishers pressing for such contributions, particularly when the text brings a practical, and novel 'how to' message to potential practitioner readers. The blurb on the cover of this (ostensible) new addition to the oeuvre will be proclaimed a 'must read' by seemingly magisterial voices in the field.

From a critical perspective it could be claimed that such texts implicitly legitimise the practice of coaching in business settings, and that many of the more instrumental examples of such literature, sourced from the University of Heathrow, could be seen as reinforcing the neoliberal, managerial discourses that underlie such legitimation. The critical gaze would proceed to challenge how some self-styled scholar-practitioners could claim to see their 'profession' from every perspective, including the critical perspective, when they are implicitly entangled in the process of reinforcing commercial imperatives within the process of professionalisation. Wrapped up in the professionalisation discourse reside the many claims made for the establishment of a viable 'evidence base', where those coming from practice would claim to have the inside track on evidence, while often seeming blind to the tendency to 'confirmation bias' often implicit in professionalizing aspects of practice.

At least one professional association expresses the urgent need to 'bridge the gap' between the academy and practice. This feeds the discourse that the academy is becoming abstracted from the day-to-day knowledge needs of those in practice and their clients, who become increasingly frustrated with the arcane theorizing of the academy. This frustration is particularly evident when the academy adopts a ideological stance, which the critical management studies (CMS) population is often accused of doing, suggesting that many critical academics write from a place that is dislocated from experience and are not engaged as practitioners.

By contrast, given the abundance of scholar-practitioners that emerge from practice, there seems little evidence of traffic in the other direction, where critical academics step into practice. If such academics exist, then the assumption would be that an academically foregrounded scholar-practitioner would be seeking peer reviewed journal publication for recognition rather than instrumental books that speak to training or advancing practice, and professionalization of the same. There are of course scholarly works on coaching, some of them critical, many of them instrumental, but few of these authors overplay a practitioner- scholar dual identity. This would lead to the conclusion that practitioners are far more ready to claim academic identity than academics are to claim the practitioner mantle.

There is little doubt that business schools and coaching associations have a part to play in the manufacturing of scholar- practitioners. Students cry out for teachers that have 'real world' stories to tell, while the business schools in their rush towards 'research – intensification,' wish to progress such practitioners towards academic respectability through engagement with evidence based, high impact inquiries that yield a professional doctorate. Business Schools can also fulfil wider university requirements for both cash and for widening participation with regional business. Individual coaches meanwhile who feel that they have hit the credentials ceiling through attaining 'mastery,' can reach beyond this end-state accreditation by reaching for the appellation of a masters or doctorate that would elevate them to a different level of competence and authority in the eyes of the world.

The rise of bullshit jobs within coaching associations

The creation of bullshit jobs is often a consequence of bureaucratic structures and hierarchies within organisations. As executives climb the corporate ladder, their influence expands, resulting in the creation of unnecessary positions to maintain hierarchical power dynamics. This perpetuates a cycle where executives commission roles that serve their interests but offer little real value to the organisation.

Maintaining a positive perception and image both internally and externally is crucial for executives. Bullshit jobs can function as tools for showcasing a perceived workforce expansion or facilitate the presentation of executives as busy and productive individuals. These roles may serve to create an illusion of growth, stability, or innovation, thereby enhancing the reputation of executives and executive coaching bodies.

The lack of clarity and uniformity in defining job roles and responsibilities plays a significant role in the prevalence of bullshit jobs. This ambiguity allows for the creation of positions that lack substantive purpose, contributing to the proliferation of redundant and meaningless roles within organisations.

More and more over recent years, coaching associations have created a proliferation of so-called "bullshit jobs," in line with the growth of such jobs in the corporate and public service sectors that they serve. These positions often confuse and bemuse regular association members, perceiving these roles to be lacking in meaningful contribution and characterised by excessive bureaucracy or lack of purpose, which in turn raises questions about the integrity and efficacy of an associations making such appointments, beyond the lure of adhering to contemporary fads and fashions.

One driving factor behind the prevalence of these bullshit jobs could lie in the association's executives' desire for personal validation and status. Consequently, executives may create unnecessary roles for themselves or their colleagues to reinforce their importance and expertise, conferring on each other grandiose titles, even if the specific responsibilities of these positions are questionable. When leaders are confronted with the need to adapt to new or uncertain circumstances, they may resort to creating meaningless roles as a way to deflect attention or delay meaningful change. By occupying their time with pseudo-responsibilities, executives can avoid addressing genuine challenges and sidestep accountability.

By creating ambiguous roles for themselves, executive can escape scrutiny and avoid being held responsible for their actions or impact. Customising roles to sound important provides these executives with an illusory sense of worth and affirms their status as indispensable members of their own leadership team, and enhances their profile and legitimacy in the eyes of prospective clients and their client organisations – and in the eyes of future employers.

The lack of a clear framework for evaluating success fosters an environment where superfluous roles can flourish. When executives shift their attention to self-serving positions rather than simply getting on with the job, their expertise and genuine value are compromised. By diverting time and resources away from supporting members and developing coaching practices and towards meaningless jobs, the overall effectiveness coaching associations erodes, leading to disillusioned members and stakeholders. This deflection takes members eyes away from hollowness of the enterprise for a while, though it does not take too long before the house of cards is seen through. The allure of performative titles and a lack of accountability encourage their creation means that these executives simply cannot resist the signifiers, especially when rival associations and corporate clients are engaged in the self-same construction of similarly titled bullshit jobs.

It is suggested here that a degree of collusion – conscious or not - between executives and coaching associations leaders perpetuates the notion that occupying high-status positions is synonymous with success and expertise. By engaging executive coaching services tied to certain prestigious sounding coaching associations, executives can bolster their sense of self and signal their significance within the corporate world. This collaboration legitimises and reinforces the existence of bullshit jobs, making them appear essential for career progression and corporate success – and cementing the need for a coach to support this success in the process, in a reinforcing loop.

The extensive collusion between executives and coaching associations leaders often occurs in environments where transparency and accountability are inadequate. This lack of oversight allows coaching associations to create programs that cater to executive demand for rapid results and minimal disruption, rather than focusing on genuine personal and professional development. This symbiotic relationship between clients and coaching associations may lead to a disregard for genuine organisational improvement and the betterment of society, or indeed without significantly contributing to the development of the coaching association complicit in this regard. Many coaching associations executive positions, despite their grand titles, arguably contribute little functionally to the organisation's overall goals, lack purpose, and perhaps offer little fulfilment to those occupying them, as they recognise the hollowness behind the title.

This close relationship between clients and association executives can also serve as a two-way transitional career bridge for executives to transition into coaching, and vice versa. In similar fashion, association executives may be offered roles in training and accreditation providers, including business schools. There is also evidence of two way traffic here also, where providers accede to roles in associations.

Fear of intimacy and of unknowing

It may be argued that executive coaching, while promising to address client's self-actualisation needs through 'unlocking of potential and' primarily caters to more fundamental requirements as outlined in Maslow's hierarchy. This claim is reinforced by evidence that professional associations often engage in pushing coaching support services and presenting them as vehicles for self-actualisation, while catering for more basic human needs.

It is axiomatic that executive coaching promises to unlock an individual's untapped potential, enabling them to excel professionally and personally, assisting clients in living 'their best lives.' Through a process of tailored guidance, coaches aim to help executives reach the pinnacle of Maslow's hierarchy - self-actualisation. This level refers to fulfilling one's own unique potential, achieving personal growth, and experiencing a sense of purpose and fulfilment. It is argued here that, contrary to the claim of self-actualisation, the lived experience of executive coaching as practiced focuses on more fundamental levels of Maslow's hierarchy, through addressing core psychological needs such as esteem, belongingness, and safety, While these aspects contribute to personal development, they do not directly address self-actualisation.

To attract members and maintain a positive reputation, professional associations frequently emphasis on self-actualisation as part of 'their DNA,' creating an aspirational expectation. This validation and recognition at a fundamental human level serves as important motivators to reinforce an individual's sense of self-worth. However, despite the fundamental role that intimacy and safety plays in personal growth and self-actualisation, it is rarely mentioned in the marketing strategies of coaching associations. Intimacy involves establishing deep emotional connections, fostering trust, and providing a space for vulnerability. As coaches and clients engage in a relationship of trust and support, it is through intimacy that true personal growth and self-actualisation can occur.

Sadly, the suppression of intimacy in coaching marketing strategies can be attributed to multiple factors. Firstly, the professional associations in the marketing of their services may prioritise the more tangible and easily marketable aspects of coaching, at the expense of mentioning of offering an intimate space, which is a more intangible and sensitive concept to promote, as it involves the sharing of personal experiences and emotions. Additionally, there may be a fear that emphasising intimacy could deter potential clients, as it requires a willingness to be vulnerable and confront personal challenges. By downplaying the need for intimacy, coaching associations may inadvertently cater to the desire for immediate results and the perception of coaching as a quick fix solution to career challenges.

The contradiction between the appeal of professional coaching association in satisfying a covert, suppressed desires for intimacy and the formal codes of ethics and conduct they uphold serve needs to be unpacked. While the need for professional integrity demands appropriate boundaries and impartiality, acknowledging and addressing the human desire for emotional closeness may well unleash the shadow side of humanness that cuts across rational ethical considerations.

It is not easy for coaches to firstly recognise this tension, and then navigate it ethically, striving to strike a balance that preserves professionalism while acknowledging and meeting their client's innate need for connection. It is the case for many coaches that -while their codes of ethics and conduct require that they adhere to rigorous formalities which implicitly forbid intimacy on any level – that they find themselves attracted to coaching predominantly due to an innate human need for connection and emotional closeness. Indeed, this need for empathic closeness is often described by some coaches as a 'vocation,' a calling, that they will follow, even if it runs up against formulated codes of conduct.

However, these codes emphasise maintaining professional boundaries, impartiality, and the avoidance of any form of intimacy that might breach ethical standards. Coaches are expected to create respectful and impartial spaces for their clients, focusing solely on helping them achieve their goals. While such guidelines are essential for preserving professional integrity, they inadvertently suppress the natural human inclination for emotional closeness, creating a contradiction within the coaching profession. The codes require a rather unrealistic demand to suppress hidden thoughts or desires; and for the coach to disengage from client encounters that excite such emotions.

The forbidden nature of intimacy in coaching relationships sparks a tension between the expectations outlined by professional coaching associations and the genuine human need for connection. Clients often seek out coaches who can provide emotional support, empathy, and understanding during their personal and professional journeys, rather than those that reinforce managerial precepts. Similarly, coaches themselves may find solace and fulfilment in forming genuine connections as they assist clients in reaching their full potential. It is of interest that while codes supervise intimate relationships between coaches and their clients, there is no evidence of reciprocal codes relating to the managing of intimacy boundaries between coaching bodies and their members, and their provider organisations? One might think that the same principles should apply across the board, as the two sides of the same coin.

With regard to valorising the quality of 'unknowing,' it is somewhat paradoxical that coaching associations might expect their members to emanate traits such as humility, vulnerability, and a sense of not knowing, while rarely showcasing these qualities themselves. This apparent contradiction raises fundamental questions about the authenticity and effectiveness of coaching practices.

Coaching is often perceived as a transformative practice that aims to unlock the potential of individuals or teams. Coaches are expected to guide others towards self-awareness, growth, and improved performance. Humility plays a crucial role in this process as it allows coaches to let go of their ego, acknowledge their limitations, and approach their clients with a non-judgmental mindset. Vulnerability is also essential, as it encourages open and honest communication, strengthens trust, and fosters deeper connections. Similarly, a sense of not knowing creates an environment of curiosity and adaptive learning, where coaches embrace uncertainty and willingly explore new frameworks or ideas.

However, the paradox emerges when observing coaching association themselves. It is not uncommon to witness coaches who prioritise asserting expertise or maintaining a façade of knowledge over embracing humility and acknowledging their own limitations. Some coaches may adopt a superior attitude, emphasising their qualifications, achievements, or experience to establish themselves as authorities in their field. By doing so, they undermine the very essence of humility, blurring the line between coaching and ego-driven mentorship.

Furthermore, the notion of vulnerability tends to be overlooked within coaching associations. Coaches are expected to have all the answers, to radiate confidence, and to project an aura of certainty. This expectation can hinder the creation of a safe space for clients to express their doubts, fears, or insecurities. When coaches refuse to admit their own vulnerabilities, they miss an opportunity to build stronger connections and foster an atmosphere of authenticity and empathy. Equally concerning is the lack of embracing for the sense of not knowing within coaching associations. They often operate within predetermined frameworks or models, adhering to a standardised approach that may not always fit the unique needs of individual clients. This rigidity can hinder coaches from exploring alternative perspectives, limiting their ability to genuinely adapt and grow alongside their clients, whose perspectives and experiences are an indispensable part of the exchange.

In a manner similar to humility, vulnerability is an essential characteristic that promotes trust and connection between a coach and their clients. Coaches who are willing to be vulnerable create a safe space for clients to share their thoughts and emotions openly. However, many coaches operate behind a façade of invulnerability, fearing that showing any vulnerability may undermine their credibility. This approach creates a barrier between the coach and client, inhibiting the formation of a genuine and trusting relationship. Coaches should understand that vulnerability is a strength that builds bridges and fosters deeper connections.

The notion of "not knowing" also plays a significant role in coaching. It is an acknowledgment that the coach does not possess all the solutions and encourages curiosity, exploration, and learning together with the client. However, many coaches feel compelled to appear knowledgeable and competent at all times. This mindset can limit their ability to truly listen to their clients, shutting down possibilities for co-creation and innovation. Embracing the concept of "not knowing" allows coaches to be more receptive to diverse perspectives and fosters a collaborative approach towards problem-solving.

In critically discussing this paradox, it is crucial to note that not all coaches exhibit these shortcomings. There are exceptional coaches who genuinely embrace humility, vulnerability, and a sense of not knowing. Their commitment to personal growth and reflection enables them to continuously improve their coaching skills and create transformative experiences for their clients - and the coaching associations should be prepared to learn from their members , not to discount them.

Jumping on the virtue signalling and greenwashing bandwagons

Virtue signalling refers to the act of making public displays or statements intended to convey moral superiority or alignment with certain values, often without substantial actions to support those claims. In the context of executive coaching, this might involve coaching associations claiming to prioritise certain values, such as sustainability, diversity, equal opportunities or social responsibility, without whole heartedly implementing practices or measures that reflect these values.

There is undoubtedly evidence that across the associations, many claims are being made for engagement with efforts supporting environmental awareness, and supporting initiatives to promote diversity and inclusivity, or support for social causes. The ICF for example, offers 'Diversity, Equity, Inclusion and Belonging at ICF.' A Scan of EMCC recent blogs includes the following topics

Hidden in plain sight: Institutional whiteness in executive coaching
Affirmations for inclusive mentors, coaches and supervisors
(3)

A conversation about coaching and diversity in organisations
Women in leadership face ageism at every age
Loneliness, belonging and inclusion

the association for coaching aims to 'make a sustainable difference to businesses, individuals, and society, worldwide. We are striving to inspire our community at all times and to engage them to create an impact on individuals, businesses, and society in general.'

On the surface, then, all of these intentions seem quite laudable. The test as to whether these coaching association genuinely prioritise these values or is engaging in virtue signalling, consider should be given to assessing whether the coaching association's actions align with the values they claim to prioritise, through transparent and consistent actions indicate a genuine commitment that go beyond marketing claims, through factors such as whether they invest resources, time, and expertise into these areas, and whether they actively seek to educate and engage both their coaches and clients in supporting the stated values.

Greenwashing refers to the act of misleadingly promoting an environmentally-friendly image or portraying false claims of sustainability without substantial actions to support it.

In the coaching industry, there may be instances where certain coaches or coaching associations might use sustainability or climate-conscious messaging as a marketing tool without genuinely incorporating sustainable practices in their operations. This can be seen in instances where coaches claim to be sustainability or eco-coaches without having the necessary knowledge or expertise in the field. It is important to assess the credibility and actions of coaches or coaching associations before engaging with them to ensure they are genuinely committed to sustainable practices.

What is of interest is that, across the bodies, there is evidence of a recent embracing of planetary purpose, which brings with it a quite alternative set of assumptions that are at variance with neofeudalistic practice. This new direction could be seen by the cynically minded as an example greenwashing, or what Rhodes has recently described as 'woke capitalism,' where a corporate declares allegiance with fashionable trends, without changing fundamental structures and practices. For others, such as those following Western's advocacy of the 'network discourse' in coaching, the embracing of coaching leaders to act in, 'good faith, to create the good society,' then this alternative direction is not an option. Perhaps it is too early to know how this embracing of purpose will pan out. One can only hope.

Decline, renewal and reinvention.

Is it possible, then, to neatly summarise the state of play for professional coaching associations? This essay began by cataloguing coaching institutes' early pushes for professionalisation, commensurate with that of professional characteristics of long-established professions. From all that we have discovered, the answer to the question is simply that professional embedding of coaching has proven impossible - nor is it ever likely to eventuate - given the fatal flaw that it is never likely that external regulation could be imposed on coaching, given the diverse nature of a sprawling market displaying various degrees of ethicality. There will always be cowboys – and some of those cowboys might just prove healthily disruptive. More recent studies suggest that while the possibility of external regulation is vanishingly thin, and the boundary around professionalism impossibly porous, it is still possible to define coaching as a 'practice' rather than a profession.

This is not a counsel of despair, as there is little sign of this practice in its many forms declining. It remains a multi-billion dollar industry which many operators still wish to capitalise upon, some benignly, some less so. It is likely the professional association landscape will remain fractured and entangled, with the old order butting up against the emergent, while celebrities and messiahs will undoubtedly seek their moment of fame. Sunk cost arguments would suggest that members will continue to cling to their chosen associations unless implosion or contamination by association suggest it is best to abandon ship.

The allure of the shiny and new will remain ever present, in a world where novelty usurps reflection. The push for global coaching may well take off and change the entire landscape – while AI in a more sophisticated form may supplant some of the more rudimentary skills of questions once exclusive to the embodied coach. Coaching associations will continue to be deeply influenced by trends in the coaching market, just as they like to continue to exert influence on the market, existing in a reciprocal push – pull dynamic.

The most likely constant in all of this will remain the deeply seated human need among coaches - either part-time or full-time, internal or external to the organisation – to seek each other out and to bond together for support, affiliation and to some degree for recognition. Enduring feedback from coaches who have come together informally or through more formal channels has been that one of the greatest benefits accrued from participation in such events has been in having the opportunity to offer each other support, affirmation and insight. Alongside this need for intimacy – though coaches would not always speak its name – resides the corresponding need for affiliation, for identity within a group. And somewhere among all the road rests the complementary needs for some humans to control, to have power, and for others to be controlled. While it is difficult to predict how coaching associations will be shaped in the future, if indeed they do survive at all, it is highly unlikely that these fundamental needs will go away. They will continue to present themselves cursively, in ever repeating circles, seeking forms to contain them.